choosing a GOOD ROAD

ISBN-13: 978-0-615-53701-6

Good Road Publishing
61 Renato Court 21B
Redwood City, CA 94061
USA

For additional resources, visit www.agoodroad.com

E-Reader download available at www.agoodroad.com

Cover Illustration by John Mavroudis

Cover and Book Design by Michael Read

These photographs are used by permission from iStockphoto.com.
Page 3 ©iStockphoto.com/eyeidea
Pages 9/51/62/75/99/127/149/179/200/221 ©iStockphoto.com/Mlenny
Pages 25/56/82/110/139/163/189/211/231 ©iStockphoto.com/PaulMaguire
Page 29 ©iStockphoto.com/ddbell
Pages 35/232 ©iStockphoto.com/fotosipsak
Page 57 ©iStockphoto.com/Adventure_Photo
Page 85 ©iStockphoto.com/mikedabell
Page 111 ©iStockphoto.com/gioadventures
Page 141 ©iStockphoto.com/BremecR
Page 147 ©Dreamstime.com/Leremy
Page 165 ©iStockphoto.com/fotoVoyager
Pages xiii/1/7/17/23/34/40/191/inside back cover ©iStockphoto.com/clintspencer
Page 213 ©iStockphoto.com/gioadventures

Dedication

This book is dedicated to my deeply loving and supportive wife, and to my children. I have learned, and continue to learn, so much from you all.

Testimonials

This is a fantastic new textbook. It is truly inspiring and motivating and provides a meaningful experience for teachers and students to share, a great fit for an advisory program! The text is engaging and strong, highlighted by the "See the Value of Failures" section, and the steps for writing a life purpose statement are so clear. The book is packed with relevant quotes, interesting "Cool Facts," opportunities to write and reflect, and an effective incorporation of cartoons, comics, and sketches. I'm a big fan of the "Never Give Up!" sections.

— Gaby DiMuro, Humanities Teacher, The Girls' Middle School, CA

Dr. Brennan has amassed a dynamic tool chest of learning modalities for students in middle school and beyond. The broad spectrum of examples and exercises allows students the opportunity to explore different learning styles and achieve individual success. The book is filled with vivid visual aids, thought-provoking questions and numerous methods that each student can use to comprehend and express themselves. Choosing a Good Road is inclusive and lively. I am definitely inspired by the techniques derived from it and I look forward to sharing them with my students. Excellent book!

— Rosetta Saunders, Middle School History Teacher, Menlo School, CA

The text is great! The focus on myelin and the notion that the brain can be "trained" and behaviors/skills can be enhanced through practice is the most crucial part of the text. "Ideas in Action" offers students a chance to dissect decisions made by others. The writing style, pace, vocabulary and organization are all spot-on.

— Dan Seder, Principal, Bay Middle College, MI

Jonathan Brennan brings so much heart, knowledge and experience through this engaging book! What a gift it is to students and teachers, providing an interactive opportunity to learn life skills that have immediate application and lasting value. Jonathan teaches skills even many adults never learn - or don't learn until much later in life, often when they're finally motivated by the pain of failure. This book promises to impart practical skills that not only guarantee greater success in the classroom, but in life. It delivers, in a fun and memorable way! Long after other textbook facts have faded, the skills and wisdom in this book will live on in each student.

— Don Fergusson, former President, Rust-Oleum Corporation

Choosing a Good Road *is a comprehensive guide for learning. It combines elements of science, language arts, history, diversity, creativity and sports in a format that will excite students and motivate teachers. The creative and innovative teacher will be able to adapt each lesson to almost any grade level.*

— Dr. Lee Mahon, Professor, Fielding Graduate University & Santa Clara University, CA (former teacher and administrator, K-12)

Jonathan Brennan's book, Choosing A Good Road, *will truly benefit students enrolled in Upward Bound programs. The knowledge and strategies outlined in this hands-on book will assist first generation college bound students with a skill set of tools that will enhance their college preparation. As a former Upward Bound Counselor at San Jose State University...I only wish this book was available for my students.* Choosing A Good Road *is a book designed to motivate and provide students with a path to college and beyond.*

— Donnelle McGee, Counselor, Mission College, CA

We have so many students who really have no idea how to set goals, identify their personal talents and interests, and chart a life course. This is a wonderful tool to help them do this. The text is very user friendly, readable with good practice exercises throughout. I really like the "Park the Judge" component—especially valuable for upper middle school students and those with self image problems. The peer pressure section is excellent and teaching students to use "I" statements is extremely valuable. There's a good lead up to problem solving and the critical thinking section uses practical, real life examples, and contemporary situations.

— Marcia Slater, retired Teacher, Principal, & Superintendent, Kent School District, WA

If your goal is increasing academic resiliency, students' ability to effectively deal with setback, stress or pressure in the academic setting, then I have found no better single source of material or text more effective than Jonathan Brennan's Choosing a Good Road.

—Philip Trejo, National School Turnaround Consultant, former Middle and High School Principal, Director of Faculty Professional Development and Gateway to College Instructor, Pueblo, CO

The Book Crew

A national expert in high school and college student success, **Dr. JONATHAN BRENNAN** holds graduate degrees in psychology, English, ethnic studies and education. He is the author of two previous books, has taught both high school and community college students, and has presented student success workshops to thousands of high school and college educators. He is the chair of the On Course National Conference, an effectiveness coach for peak performers, and father of two children in middle and high school.

SYDNEY DELP, from Hermantown, Minnesota, is currently a student at Carleton College studying physics and political science. She became a doodler after admiring the cartoons her father drew religiously on her lunch bags and excelled as a doodler during four years of turning in highly decorated math assignments. Her interests include horses, deep thinking and music, and you can see more at www.facebook.com/Sydney.Delp.

KHALID BIRDSONG is a freelance cartoonist and art teacher in Northern California. He is the writer and artist of the humorous webcomic "Fried Chicken and Sushi," based on his two years living in Osaka, Japan. Khalid enjoys teaching art to kindergarten through sixth grade at a private school in Palo Alto. In his free time, he loves to spend time with his wife and daughter and travel the world. You can check out his work at www.ksbirdsong.blogspot.com and read his comic at www.friedchickenandsushi.com.

Over nearly two decades, **MICHAEL READ** has published numerous books, magazines, newsletters, travel guides and websites. Michael is the Publications Director of the San Francisco Film Society, and has served as editor of four books of fine art photography, as graphic designer of nine more, and editor of magazines including see: a journal of visual culture and **Release Print**. He holds an MFA in Photography from the School of Visual Arts in New York.

JOHN MAVROUDIS, the cover artist and one of the book illustrators, lives in San Francisco. He's been a DJ at a Rock & Roll station, worked on a presidential campaign, designed a cover for the New Yorker that won Magazine Cover of the Year, and has created numerous CD and concert poster designs which you can view at his website, www.zenpop.com.

Acknowledgments

My deepest appreciation to the late Fernando Tolivar, singer, inventor, aerospace engineer, master of paella and the loving *abuelo* of my children. I miss you.

I'd like to extend my appreciation and thanks to the many reviewers of this textbook. Your contributions, ideas, feedback, suggestions, support and wisdom have been invaluable. You are extraordinary educators. Any errors that remain in the book are mine.

Much thanks to Lee Mahon, Susan McCaffrey, Susan Hass, Eve Kikawa, Suz Antink, Noushin Bayat, Don Fergusson, Eileen Zamora, Deborah Shulman, Alissa Picker, Donnelle McGee, Rob Jenkins, Denise Dufek, Richard Kiefer, Nancy Brennan, Peter Brennan, and many others who provided feedback and direction.

Thanks as well to the illustrators, Sydney Delp, John Mavroudis and Khalid Birdsong, and the tireless and talented book designer, Michael Read. My grateful appreciation for Eileen and your excellent feedback and guidance (and humor!).

I'd also like to thank Dr. Skip Downing for his extraordinary vision, friendship and wisdom. Thanks for helping me stay on course.

Also thanks to my colleagues Yolanda and David Coleman, Ray Charland, Dave Ellis, Pete Chandonnet, Barbara Whiteside, and all of the many educators who have shared their ideas and strategies with me.

My biggest thanks to the thousands of students who have shared their wisdom with me. I'm still learning from all of you.

The Purpose of Choosing a Good Road

❶ The purpose of the *Choosing a Good Road* textbook is to give students the tools they need to succeed in high school and be ready for college and career.

THE PROBLEM: Graduation rates from high schools in the United States are frustratingly low and schools have major challenges in promoting student effectiveness.

- Fewer than 70% of students graduate from high school

- 48% or fewer graduate in the 50 largest school districts

- The achievement gap for at-risk students: graduation rates well below 50%

Students who do graduate are often not well prepared for college and the workplace. The challenges are enormous and require a fresh approach.

SOLUTIONS: The ***Choosing a Good Road*** textbook offers middle & high school students:

- 36 Learning Skills to Improve Learning Outcomes

- 9 Effectiveness Skills to Increase Student Performance

- Brain-Based Strategies to Promote Active Learning

- Life Purpose & Mission Statement Activities

- A Framework for Setting Life & Learning Goals

- An Opportunity to Clarify & Apply Personal Values

- Methods to Shift Negative Beliefs to More Productive Mindsets

- More Effective Peer Pressure & Positive Assertiveness Skills

- Systems to Enhance Organization & Efficiency

- Creative & Critical Thinking Approaches for Better Problem Solving

- Diversity Awareness & Management Strategies

- Leadership & Communication Tools

- Mindfulness Practices & Improved Focus Skills

2 **The purpose of the Choosing a Good Road Workshop is to give middle and high school educators the tools they need to help students succeed in high school and be ready for college and career.**

The Choosing a Good Road Workshop for middle and high school teachers, counselors and administrators, is an active learning experience that offers proven strategies in learner effectiveness. Educators learn the tools required to dramatically increase high school completion rates and college/career readiness. Workshop strategies are drawn from the work of leading researchers in multiple fields of learner effectiveness.

Educators acquire best practices in:

- Classroom Management Skills & Designing/Facilitating Learner-Centered Education

- Brain-Based Research & Multiple Learning Skills

- Learner Motivation, Academic Goal Setting, Autonomous Learning & Achievement

- Emotional Effectiveness, Leadership Strategies & Organization & Efficiency Practices

- Effectiveness Skills to Empower Students to Make Better Choices as Learners

- Communication Skills, Revising Limiting Beliefs, & Improving Self Efficacy

- Promoting Critical & Creative Thinking & Using Problem-Based Learning

Educators leave the workshop knowing what it takes for their students to become peak performers in high school (and become college/career ready). They learn how to support students in making more effective choices.

I like how the workshop is designed to work in so many ways. The information can help you personally and professionally. You stop and think about yourself and then how you can use this information to help others. Lots of great stuff!

—April Johnson, Counselor, Willamina High School, OR

You are facilitating what you are trying to get across to others. I realized how much we covered when I started writing down all the new tools.

—Chris Daniels, Principal, Amity High School, OR

The intended workshop result is to give educators the tools to increase student retention, graduation and college enrollment rates. It also provides tools for educators to prepare students for the workplace and to promote deeper and more long-lasting student learning.

③ The purpose of the website (www.agoodroad.com) is to provide additional resources for students and educators.

The website features additional resources for both students and educators, and it is constantly evolving, with new materials added every month. If you have any suggestions (or requests), please contact success@agoodroad.com.

Choosing a Good Road Intervention Models

How can Choosing a Good Road be used with students?

The textbook can be used in numerous student success models. Content can be taught in a single life-skills course, embedded in a single course from a core discipline like English or mathematics, or infused across the school curriculum, in face-to-face or online settings. These models include:

— **Stand-Alone Success Classes**
— **Orientation/Bridge Programs & Workshops**
— **Linked Courses and Learning Communities**
— **Success-Infused Single Discipline Courses**
— **Success-Infused Multi-Discipline Courses**
— **Success Across the Curriculum Programs**
— **Before or After-School Classes & Programs**
— **Distance Education Success Program Delivery Models**
— **Your School's Innovative Model**

If you'd like support in developing methods to introduce these skills to your students (and educators), please contact us through the website and we'd be glad to share both research and success program development strategies.

Textbook Features

Preview Questions At the beginning of each chapter there are preview questions that get students thinking right away.

9 Effectiveness Skills and Activities Every chapter includes an explanation of one of the nine effectiveness skills. In order to promote active learning, students are asked to practice these skills in the chapter activities. The effectiveness skills are evidence-based learner and life skills that provide students the foundation they need to succeed in high school.

What's the Point? Students are frequently asked to reflect on what they've just read in order to sharpen their critical thinking skills (and solidify their learning). This feature offers practice in finding and clarifying main points.

Cool Facts Students are invited to stay engaged by reading interesting brief facts about the chapter's topic.

Road Log This feature invites students to create a blog or online journal that documents their journey down a good road. Students have the option to write on the textbook pages or to use the Road Log to record their ideas on their computer.

36 Learning Skills Every chapter offers students an opportunity to understand three different learning skills. Developed from validated assessments and psychological typing tests, the learning skills are a reflection of the multiplicity of approaches used by learners. Students will review their most effective strategies recorded in these skills, as well as new approaches.

Ideas in Action Using a problem-based learning format, students are given a chance to explore a "real-life" student challenge, and to suggest solutions based on the skills they have been learning.

Maga and Keya on A Good Road Maga and Keya are two fictional Lakota Indian superheroes who appear in each chapter. In this graphic novel-style drama, Maga and Keya struggle against the forces that try to push them off the good road they are traveling. They practice and promote the skills presented in every chapter.

Ready for College This feature is based on recent research on the skills, attitudes and competencies required to prepare students for college. Students have a chance to learn, then practice what they need to know (and do) to prepare for college. All students should have an opportunity to be well prepared for college so that they can then make an informed and empowered decision when they reach this critical crossroad in their lives.

Ready for Career Students also deserve the chance to learn what they need to know to excel in their careers. They'll learn skills they can put to use in their current employment, upon completing high school, while working during college, or after they've acquired a college degree. These skills are based on soft skills competencies researched by organizations such as the Partnership for 21st Century Skills, a national organization that advocates for 21st century readiness for every student (www.p21.org). These competencies are in high demand by employers.

Life & Lyrics Integrating music and effectiveness skills, this feature invites students to listen to songs, answer questions, and discover valuable lessons. It reinforces concepts and strategies from each chapter and embeds them in activities that students find compelling and fun.

What Did You Learn? At the end of each chapter, students are asked to reflect on their most important learning from the chapter concepts and activities.

Never Give Up!!! This is perhaps the single most important concept in the entire book. Students learn a series of strategies that will help them persist until they reach their most important academic and life goals.

TABLE OF CONTENTS

Chapter Eight: Be a Leader

Chapter Nine: Paying Attention

Conclusion: Crossroads

INTRODUCTION

 What are you waiting for? It's time to get moving to create a great life for yourself!

I know, I know. You probably already have a pretty good life. Most of you have a place to live, food to eat, clothes to wear, and family/friends who care about you. You may even have an iPod, smartphone and some stylin' footwear.

But what else? How do you get from a pretty good life to a great life? How can you be sure you graduate from high school, make it into college, and find the job you want? How do you keep making new friends, manage not to go crazy when your family is a pain, and spend most of your time being happy and excited about your life?

It's easy (kind of). You just need to keep choosing a good road. Just by opening to this page, you've taken the first step down the road to an amazing life. But there are many paths to choose in life, and so many people end up going down the wrong road. This book teaches you what you need to know to pick the right path. I hope you get what you want.

You have an opportunity to create a life that is even better than the one you have. You could even learn to really appreciate the life you have. But will you actually choose to do so? The truth is, many people don't make choices that get them what they want. Each time they arrive at a crossroads, they pick the wrong road, a road that leads them away from what they want. They keep choosing to be unhappy because they keep choosing the wrong road. It's really hard to live life like that. I think you can do better than picking the hard way to do life. In fact, I know you can do better than this. Here's why:

I waited a long time to choose a better road for myself. I made lots of mistakes. In fact, I never chose to graduate from high school. I dropped out instead. It was a big mistake. I was unhappy, confused, argued a lot with my parents, had a go-nowhere job and made many bad decisions. I kept choosing the path that took me far away from my goals and dreams. I did not use the life skills that would have made a big difference in helping me reach my dreams and goals. After many years of creating a life that I was not enjoying, I began to learn new skills, and soon I put these new skills to use. I enrolled in a community college and finally transferred to a university and completed my undergraduate and graduate degrees. As I began to make better choices, I finally started to see what was getting in my way (and it was mostly me, by the way).

Sometimes I wish I had learned all this when I was much younger. Other times I'm happy to recognize that if I hadn't done it the hard way, I wouldn't have learned so much. I understand more about why many students don't succeed, and how to help them do better in school.

Since I have such a great life, I decided to give back. For many years, I have been teaching high school and college students how to create extraordinary lives. I teach them how to dream big, set goals and take action to get what they want. I teach students the same life skills that helped me finally reach my dreams. You can learn these the hard way (like I did) or the easier way (by reading this book and trying out the tools). It's your choice.

I would like to offer my mistakes as valuable learning opportunities. I am hoping that you will choose to gain more wisdom and get what you want. Fun is optional (but recommended).

Jonathan

CHAPTER ONE

BRING ON THE LEARNING!

Read the chapter to answer these preview questions.

How do you give your brain a workout?

What is a dendrite?

What would happen if you got a lot smarter?

Are you visual? verbal? hands-on?

How do you speed up your brain?

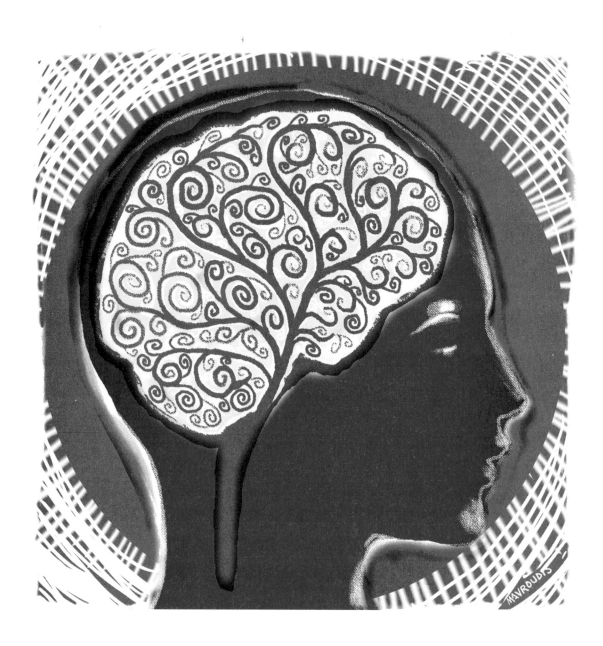

Bring On the Learning!

Ever wonder what's happening in your brain? How do you actually cram all that information in your head? How do you come up with all those ideas? Why do you think what you think? How do you get smarter at math or better at shooting hoops? Scientists have discovered a lot about what happens in our brains. Here's what's most important:

 The harder you work, the smarter you get. To become a great basketball player or excellent at solving algebra problems, you need to practice over and over.

NBA star LeBron James is not one of the league's best players because he has talent. He is a great player because he works very, very hard. His personal shooting coach, Chris Jent, says that the number of hours James practices his shots is almost unbelievable. He commits to shooting hundreds of baskets in every practice session.

Retired NBA star Michael Jordan always wanted to be in the best possible shape. He lifted weights, ate right and made sure he was in superb physical condition. He worked hard to turn his weaknesses into strengths. During the off-season, five days a week, for five hours at a time, he worked on his skills.

Retired basketball star, Lisa Leslie, won two WNBA championships, made seven All-Star appearances, and was a three-time MVP. She won four Olympic gold medals and was the first player to dunk in a WNBA game. How'd she get so good? You guessed it: hard work! She practiced in high school 3 hours a day, shooting 400 shots from all around the court during each practice session.

You're only born with a certain amount of gifts. You have to take advantage of them and put in the work. My work ethic has helped me be the player I am today.
—*LeBron James*

I'm not out there sweating for three hours every day just to find out what it feels like to sweat.
—*Michael Jordan*

It's easy to think that the basketball stars on television are just naturally great basketball players. It's more accurate to say it's because of the hard work they have put in over many years. Math is a lot like basketball. Some students just appear to be great at math. They zip through problems, quickly adding or dividing long numbers, or easily reducing fractions. But just like the basketball players, they can do this easily only because they have practiced for so many hours. You can be great at math too (and basketball), when you understand how your brain works.

Neurons are cells in your brain. You have about one hundred billion neurons. Operating like an internet cable, they send rapid signals to other **neurons** through the **synapses**, the points where neurons connect. Your brain processes information using networks built from neurons.

Math is a lot like basketball.

Dendrites are like the branches of a tree. The neurons grow these branching networks each time you use them. The more you use your brain, the more networks you grow.

✳ To understand what's happening in your brain, you need to learn about neurons, synapses and dendrites.

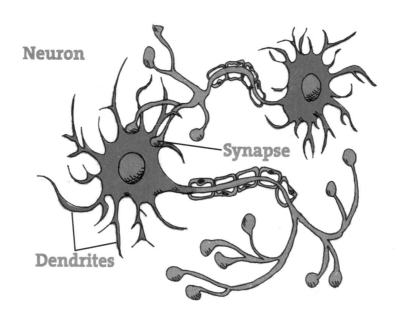

Neuron

Synapse

Dendrites

The more networks you grow, the better you can think (the "smarter" you become). You need to use your neurons to grow more neurons (to think better), and also to remember things, like how to lift a slice of pizza to your mouth, or how to kick a ball.

Cool Facts

- As a baby, you start with 100 billion **neurons** (brain cells).

- You then create 1.8 million new **synapses** per second!

- You can have 100 trillion to 1000 trillion **synapses**. You have more connections in your brain than the number of known particles in the universe.

- You must practice a new skill within two minutes of learning it, or the newly formed **dendrite** will shrivel and disappear (and you'll have to learn it again).

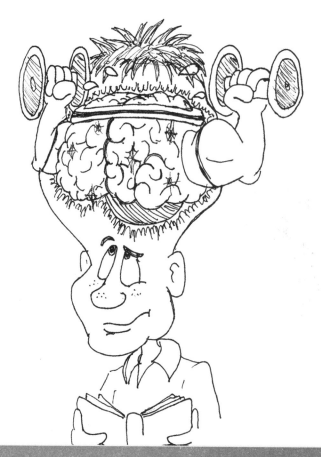

Working Out Your Brain

Weightlifters get stronger by lifting weights. They don't get stronger by watching other people lift weights, or by eating potato chips while walking past the weight room.

Math students work out their brains by solving math problems. They don't get stronger brains by watching other people solve math problems, or by eating potato chips while walking past other people who are solving math problems.

Your brain is like a big muscle. Do you want a flabby brain or a strong brain? It's your choice. Since you get smarter by working out your brain, get smarter right now by writing down this chapter's main points. Try the *What's the Point?* activity on the next page.

What's the Point?

Write down 2 main points from this chapter (here or in your Road Log).

1 ....

....

....

....

2 ....

....

....

....

....

Create Your Road Log

If your teacher doesn't want you to write on the textbook pages, log your ideas in a notebook, in a computer file, or online. To create an online Road Log, you can post on a discussion board or in a personal blog (web log) that is viewable (or not) by others. You can also try a videoblog or photoblog.

You can divide your Road Log into sections with the headings from the list to the right, or you can divide your Road Log into the 9 chapters of the textbook. Post daily or weekly by topic. Create your Road Log right now.

Preview Questions

Notes

What's the Point?

Learning Skills

Ideas in Action

Other Activities

Ready for College

Ready for Career

Life and Lyrics

Never Give Up!!!

What Did You Learn?

Three Ways to Give Your Brain a Workout

Here's how to exercise your brain:

1 The ABCs of Dendrites

A PRACTICE RIGHT AWAY.
Practice a new skill within 2 minutes or the newly formed dendrite will shrivel and disappear. Try it now with this idea.

If a new skill is not practiced, a new dendrite will shrivel within _____ minutes.

B LEARN DIFFERENT WAYS TO BUILD DENDRITES.
Students should learn about the same ideas in many different ways in order to build more dendrite connections. The more ways through which you experience ideas, the more new pathways you create in your brain. Then it's easier to access that knowledge when you need it.

You can take an idea that you just read about and then:

■ listen to or write a song

■ view or create and upload a YouTube video clip

■ draw a picture, map or flowchart

■ build a 3-dimensional model

■ stand up, move around and form a human model of the idea

Represent this new concept about learning by drawing a picture in the box below that shows a student building dendrites using at least two different methods.

C DENDRITES GROW FROM STIMULATING EXPERIENCES. You might have observed that you don't learn well when you're bored. Students must have stimulating experiences to stay engaged and motivated. Without a stimulating experience, dendrites do not grow. It would be great if teachers always provided you with a stimulating learning experience, but some do and some don't. Even teachers that often do can't *always* design something that will engage you. So you must engage yourself to keep learning well.

Without a stimulating experience, dendrites do not grow.

Describe one type of learning experience that you find stimulating and engaging (for example, a field trip).

....

....

....

② Build Myelin

Ever notice how some people seem to be really good at soccer...or writing...or singing? Ever think maybe they're just naturally good at singing, or that you might not be good at singing? It seems reasonable, but it's not true.

The myelin sheath is a layer of cells that grows on the outside of neurons. Myelin allows you to speed up your brain. The way to get myelin to build is through practicing just the right way:

 Practice a lot. It takes many hours to master a skill. Work on it every day and you will get better and better. One day you will discover that you have become an expert. Once you build layers of myelin, the signals in your brain will travel 100 times faster than before.

Myelin allows people to become better at soccer, better at solving math problems or better at any other mental or physical skill. The more myelin you have, the faster you can think and react. You can build up to 50 layers of myelin on each neuron. Once you build layers of myelin through Effective Practice, here's what happens:

The signals that travel along the neurons in your brain can increase their speed from **2 miles per hour** to **200 miles per hour**.

You can send up to **30 times more signals down the same neuron in the same time period**.

The **overall processing in your brain can become 3000 times more effective**.

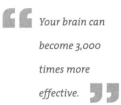

Your brain can become 3,000 times more effective.

MYELIN SHEATH: 3 RULES OF EFFECTIVE PRACTICE

BREAK IT DOWN
Break any skill down into its smaller parts:

A look at the task as a whole

B divide the task into the smallest possible chunks

C change the speed at which you practice the task:
alternately slowing down and then speeding up

PRACTICE IT
Practice the action with focus and repetition:

A practice daily or very frequently for 1 or 2+ hours

B challenge yourself at your maximum ability

C stay focused on the skill you intend to practice

SENSE IT
Pay close attention to how you're practicing:

A practice concentrating on your actions

B reach beyond your capacity, fall short and reach again

C be productive and recognize mistakes immediately

Three Learning Skills

As a VISUAL LEARNER, you learn well with images you can see, for example:

- viewing PowerPoint slideshows or websites
- looking at colorful graphics, illustrations and animations
- watching YouTube videos
- absorbing diagrams, charts and timelines
- thinking by drawing pictures

As a VERBAL LEARNER, you learn well by speaking and hearing ideas, for example:

- listening to songs and music
- presenting or hearing oral reports
- engaging in debates
- hearing experts speak about concepts
- asking questions about how to do something

As a HANDS-ON LEARNER, you learn well by doing something, for example:

- moving from one learning station to another learning station
- building a model of the concept
- taking field trips
- trying science experiments
- using objects in a lesson role play

③ Three Learning Skills: Visual, Verbal and Hands-On.

Review the three learning skills on the opposite page. Students can learn new ideas and skills in many different ways. If you understand that you have many options and learning strategies, you can use more strategies to be a better learner.

A Number the three skills as follows: 1) the skill I prefer to use most often, 2) the skill I prefer to use sometimes, and 3) the skill I prefer to use least often.

1 ....

2 ....

3 ....

B Write down an example of how you have used one of the strategies from the skill you chose as #1 . For instance, if you chose Hands-On Learner, an example might be: I built a 3-D model of the Gettysburg battlefield.

....

....

....

C Write down one way you could use one of the strategies from the skill you chose as #3. For instance, if you chose Verbal Learner, an example might be: I could bring in a song about soldiers.

....

....

....

ideas in action

It was only three weeks after the first day of high school, but Marcus already knew he wasn't doing well.

In his English class, he had failed the first 2 vocabulary tests, and his first paper was covered in teacher comments and red marks.

His math teacher asked him to stay after class to discuss his homework. She told Marcus that more than half his answers were wrong.

Even in his favorite class, American History, Marcus sometimes fell asleep and when he tried to read his notes to study for a test, he couldn't understand them.

Recommend three things Marcus could do that would help him be a better learner.

1 ....

....

....

2 ....

....

....

3 ....

....

....

Action is the real measure of intelligence.
—Napoleon Hill

Choose Your Road

If you don't like the road you're walking, start paving another one. —**Dolly Parton**

If someone is going down the wrong road, he doesn't need motivation to speed him up. What he needs is education to turn him around. —**Jim Rohn**

Sometimes the road less traveled is less traveled for a reason. —**Jerry Seinfeld**

Choose any one of the three quotes above.

A Rewrite the quote in your own words:

....

....

....

....

B Explain why the idea is important in words that you might send in an email or text message (optional to send):

....

....

....

....

Introducing
MAGA and KEYA on A Good Road

MAGA and **KEYA** are two Lakota Indian superheroes who appear in a cartoon page in every chapter. Lakota Indians are a Native American tribe with seven bands or "sub-tribes." Many Lakota live in North and South Dakota, some on reservations and others in towns and cities across the state. They also live in many other states across the country and in parts of Canada.

Maga and Keya struggle against the forces that try to push them off the good road they are walking.

Meet MAGA: Maga means "Duck" in the Lakota language. Maga has wings and can fly anywhere. She is good at staying on track and solving problems. She uses Value Shields to keep her safe from wandering off the good road. You'll learn more about Value Shields in Chapter 3.

Meet KEYA: Keya means "Turtle" in the Lakota language. Keya can run and jump over mountains (as long as he remembers to practice). He has a powerful protective shell, like a turtle. He also has a collection of Value Shields to keep him safe from wandering off the good road.

1 What do you think are the major reasons some high school students don't apply to college?

....

....

....

....

....

2 How would you advise them to move forward if they did want to attend college? What are their next steps?

....

....

....

....

....

Initiative and Self-Direction

When I was in high school, I once worked as a temporary employee on a 3-week assignment entering payments into a computer. As I worked, I noticed that there were nearly two hundred previous payment entries that were incomplete. I asked another employee what to do about them. She said, "Don't worry, they've been there forever."

I wasn't worried, but I wanted to do my best at this job. I researched the payments, and updated all the records over the next two weeks. At the end of my temporary assignment, the office manager told me that none of the full-time employees had ever taken the initiative to clear up the old payments. She was grateful and said that if I ever needed to use her as a reference, I could. I thanked her.

The next year, when I was applying for a full-time job, I asked her for a letter of recommendation. Her very strong recommendation allowed me to get both the interview and the job offer.

Initiative and Self-Direction

Why wait for someone to tell you to do something valuable? Employers want employees who are willing to get something important done or a problem solved, without being told to do it. Take initiative. Instead of being completely directed by others, be self-directed. In order to practice this, identify two unsolved problems and actions to solve them.

Problem at School (maybe the water fountain has been leaking for weeks or the library printer quit working):

....

Action to Solve Problem at School (you can ask for help):

....

....

....

....

Problem at Home (maybe your new dog keeps escaping from the back yard or your room needs a reading light):

....

Action to Solve Problem at Home:

....

....

....

....

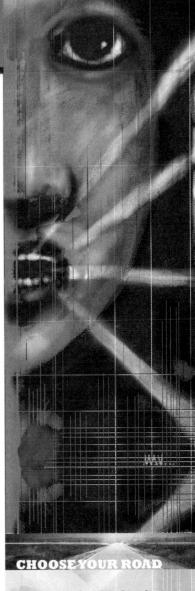

Choose a song about learning from your music library. Listen to the lyrics carefully, writing down three important points the songwriter makes about learning.

1 ....

....

2 ....

....

3 ....

....

Which important point do you agree with, and why?

....

....

....

....

....

CHOOSE YOUR ROAD

Life is one big road with lots of signs. So when you ridin' through the ruts, don't complicate your mind. Flee from hate, mischief and jealousy...

—Bob Marley

What did you learn?

I know you've learned a few important things!

❝ *The road to success is always under construction.* **❞**

—Lily Tomlin

NEVER GIVE UP!!!

See the Value of Failures

J.K. Rowling is the author of the popular *Harry Potter* book series, but her first book was rejected twelve times by publishers. Now her books have sold more than 400 million copies. Rowling says: "You might never fail on the scale I did, but some failure in life is inevitable."

Thomas Edison once had a teacher tell him he was too stupid to learn in school. He failed more than 9,000 times before he succeeded in creating the first light bulb. He would go on to create more than 1,000 innovations.

Michael Jordan was cut from his high school basketball team because of his "lack of skill." Now he is widely seen as one of the greatest basketball players of all time.

Steven Spielberg wanted to be a filmmaker but was rejected by three film schools. He would eventually win an Academy Award, become a co-founder of the DreamWorks movie studio and set records for the most widely seen films of all time, including the *Star Wars* series, *Indiana Jones*, *The Color Purple*, *Jurassic Park*, *Amistad*, and many more.

Babe Ruth struck out 1,330 times. He also hit 714 home runs in his career and is one of the most legendary baseball players of all time. After each strikeout, he knew another home run was just around the corner.

The roughest road often leads to the top.
—Christina Aguilera

Many of life's failures are people who had not realized how close they were to success when they gave up.
— Thomas Edison

Oprah Winfrey experienced many challenges during her childhood and early career. As a young girl, she was so poor that she wore potato sack dresses. As an adult, she lost her first news anchor job. Yet she would eventually become the host of the highest-rated talk show in history, CEO of a media empire, a billionaire and one of the most influential women in the world.

Abraham Lincoln lost his job, was defeated when running for the state legislature, failed in business, had a nervous breakdown, lost a nomination for Congress, lost a Senate race (twice), and then was elected President of the United States.

Failures offer many important lessons, as long as we don't give up just because we failed at something. Re-read the stories above about successful people who have experienced failure. What do you think they might have believed about failure that allowed them to keep trying until they reached their goals?

Belief: Failure is...

....

....

....

Write below something that you have "failed" at in your life. I have failed at:

....

....

....

....

What motivating belief do you think would help you keep trying to succeed in life, despite your previous failure?

Motivating Belief:

....

....

....

Cool Facts

■ People don't make good decisions when they are hungry and tired. They're not good at resisting the temptation of wasting time on the internet. They have a hard time avoiding unhealthy foods. Make important decisions early in the day, or when rested after a healthy meal.

■ Some psychologists argue that a sign of maturity is to have a clear purpose in your life. When you have purpose and goals, you have better mental health.

■ High school graduates earn almost 40% more each year than high school dropouts. College graduates with a bachelor's degree earn about $1,000,000 more than high school graduates during their entire career. A university master's degree is worth $1.3 million more in career earnings than a high school diploma. University graduates with doctoral degrees earn an average of $3.4 million during their working life.

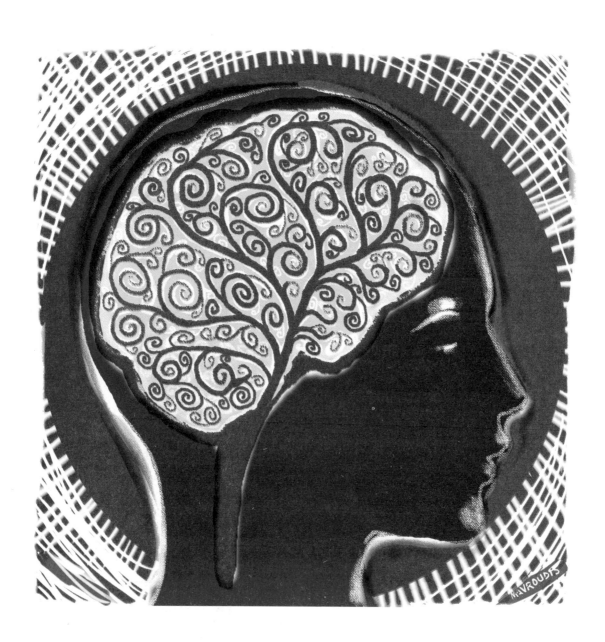

CHAPTER TWO

IT'S MY CHOICE

Read the chapter to answer these preview questions.

How would it change your life if you went to college?

Who are the Lost Boys of Sudan?

Why do you need to have a purpose to your life?

What are the Four Steps to Success?

How do you choose a good road?

It's My Choice

It's 7:30 am. It's time to leave for school. You have a report to give in history class at exactly 8 a.m. If you don't leave in 5 minutes, you won't get there on time. You're waiting for your little brother. Your little brother is yelling and screaming because he can't find his favorite shoes, and he won't wear the shoes he wore yesterday. Your mom's screaming at your brother because your brother's throwing a tantrum. Your dad's running around the house like crazy trying to find your little brother's favorite shoes. You're not happy because you need to leave for school right away.

You've got a few more minutes before you need to go out the door. What would you do? Write your choice below (for example: I run around trying to find his favorite shoes).

My choice: I would...

....

....

....

....

Believe it or not, it *is* your choice. It's true that until you're 18, when it's *all* your choice as to what you do with your life, your parents make some decisions for you. It may seem like they make a lot of them–perhaps too many, but really *you* make *most* of your life decisions.

Making good decisions is important because if you don't make good decisions, you won't get what you want. You may even get a lot of what you don't want if you make poor decisions. Even if you make good decisions, you won't *always* get what you want, but people who make good decisions get *more of what they want* in their lives. The first step in making good decisions is recognizing that *it's your choice*.

In the situation on the previous page, you might choose to do nothing (that's a choice). You might choose to yell at everyone: *"I'm gonna be late for schooooool!!!!!"* (another choice). You might head out the front door, yell *"I'm going to school!"* and jog down to the schoolbus stop. If you depend on your parents to drive, you might try to persuade one of them to take you now and take your brother later when he's ready. You might sit down and review your history report note cards so you feel more confident when you do get to history class. There are always lots of choices–even when we feel stuck in someone else's problems–even when it's really noisy because everyone's yelling.

> When life hands us a big problem, it's even more important to see that you have many choices.

If solving the problem with your little brother really *was* your choice (and not someone else's), what would you do? Remember: what you get comes from what you choose.

Write two possible choices here:

This would be a good choice for me:

....

What I would really want if I had it my way:

....

Yet some people have much bigger problems than lost shoes. When life hands us a big problem, it's even more important to see that you have many choices (even if there are some really tough ones).

The Lost Boys of Sudan

When government troops attacked villages in the African country of Sudan, they killed many villagers (close to two million people were killed in the civil war). The nearly 27,000 "Lost Boys" were left as orphans, with no parents, often separated from the rest of their families. Even though they were on their own, these boys didn't give up: they escaped the war by making long journeys that often lasted years.

Many chose to leave home and walk hundreds of miles to international relief camps in Ethiopia and Kenya. They struggled with no food, no water, burning hot weather, animal attacks and illness. Imagine the many important decisions they needed to make along the way: "How will I get more food?" "Where is it safe to sleep?" "Who can I trust?"

Thousands of these Lost Boys finally escaped the refugee camps to arrive in the United States. But what if they had waited around for someone else to take action for them? What if they had decided to give up on themselves? Who would save them if they didn't save themselves, recognizing that it was *their choices* that would make the difference between life and death?

We were left to fend for ourselves. We had to build our own houses and construct roads too. When we went to the bush to fell trees, some of our friends never returned. We left them out there, killed by lions.

—Lost Boys

Bethany Hamilton

When Bethany was 8 years old, she won first place in a surfing contest. She won two major surfing competitions the same year, then several more by age 11. She picked up a national sponsor, Rip Curl. Bethany's career as a professional surfer was on track. When Bethany was 13, while surfing off the coast of Hawaii in 2003, a shark attacked her and bit off her left arm. Bethany survived, and then faced many choices: Would she ever go in the ocean again? Would she surf again? Would she try to live a "normal" life with only one arm?

Bethany wasted no time. A few weeks after the attack, she was back on her board: "To me, it's like never getting in a car because you're afraid of a collision. Not surfing doesn't work for me," she said. Two years after the attack, Hamilton won 1st place in the NSSA National Championships, and recently, in her first adult competition, she finished third.

"One arm might handicap me a little in competition, but I just work with what changes I know I have to make, and I'm pretty used to it now," she told ABC News. "It mainly depends on the wave conditions...I only get half the waves everyone else rides, so mine have to be good!" Even though life can send us some pretty hard challenges, it's our choices that determine what happens next.

I just work with what changes I know I have to make.

—*Bethany Hamilton*

Happiness is not a destination. It is a method of life.

—Burton Hills

Whether choosing your waves or your next life goal, the decision is yours. The life you live today is mostly the result of all the decisions you have made so far. It's true that you haven't been responsible for *everything* that has happened in your life. Maybe your family decided to move from one city to another when you were three years old. You didn't make that decision. It's true that you aren't responsible for *everything*, but consider this: the more of your life you are willing to own and take action on, the more influence you can have over what you get.

For example, if your family does choose to move to another city, or you start at a new school where you know NOBODY, what you do next is your choice. You might decide to stay mad for a long time, or talk to none of those jerks at your new school, or to start playing hours of video games. You might also decide to make one new friend, talk to your Mom about how hard it is, or join the basketball team.

You might not have created the situation, but it's your choice to make decisions that change the situation, that keep it the same, or that even make it worse.

Look, if the Lost Boys or Bethany Hamilton can choose their path in the face of huge obstacles (much bigger obstacles than starting at a new school), you can keep choosing your path too. However, it's hard to choose the right path if you don't know where you're going, right? In this chapter you will learn a few new tools to help you figure out where you're going and how to keep moving in the right direction.

LIFE PURPOSE

For starters, what are you doing here? I mean, what are you doing on this planet? Ever thought about that? My discovery has been that all of us have a purpose in our lives, but not everyone takes the time to figure out what it is. Imagine that you are waiting in a long line at your favorite ice cream place. It takes forever to get to the front of the line, and in the meantime you watch everyone else gobbling down their favorite flavors (chocolate fudge, mint chip, strawberry...). At last, you get to the front of the line, and they ask you what you want. Ummmmmm. Ummmmm. Hmmmmm. (You think: "I don't really know. How could I forget what I like?") You stall for time: "Could I try the cookie crunch?" You finish the tiny sample on the spoon...hmmmmm.... uhhhhhhhhh (you stall for some more time): "Could I try the raspberry vanilla swirl?"

"OK," says the ice cream clerk, "You only get two taste spoons. What do you want?" "I don't know," you say. She tells you, "Sorry, there's a long line of people behind you. If you don't know what you want, you'll have to go back to the end of the line. Or I could just give you my favorite flavor, peanut butter broccoli olive oil tofu crunch with bitter lemon sprinkles?" You say, "Forget it," walking out of the ice cream store. This is lame. *How could you forget what you really want?*

Some people have no idea what they're doing here. They don't know why they're on the earth. It's as though they walked up to the counter of life and forgot what they wanted to ask for. When you do this, you either get sent to the back of the line to start over, missing a great opportunity, or someone else decides what you get in life. You might think you'd never forget your favorite flavor, but is it possible you don't know the purpose of your life? You need to know what your purpose is, so you know what you want and can then take action to go get it.

Mission Statement

Most companies have a purpose; it's their mission statement. This statement is supposed to capture the basic purpose of the company or organization. The Humane Society has a special project called Mission: Humane. Their goal is to "Get young people involved in animal protection" and prevent the abuse of animals. Here's their mission:

"MISSION: HUMANE GETS YOUNG PEOPLE ACTIVELY INVOLVED IN ANIMAL PROTECTION AND PROVIDES RESOURCES FOR CLASSROOM TEACHERS, ANIMAL SHELTERING PROFESSIONALS, AND OTHERS TO GUIDE YOUTH ANIMAL PROTECTION CLUBS."

In-N-Out Burger has this mission statement: "Give customers the freshest, highest quality foods you can buy and provide them with friendly service in a sparkling clean environment."

Your mission statement helps you remember what's important. It helps you decide if you're going in the right direction. The Humane Society knows that animal protection is their purpose, while In-N-Out Burger knows that providing fresh and high quality food is their purpose. What's your mission statement? What's your purpose? What's your passion? What direction are you heading in your life?

Writing Your Life Purpose

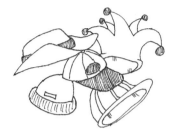

A life purpose statement is similar to a company's mission statement. It's your personal mission statement. Consider some of the many hats you wear in life (student, daughter/son, friend, basketball player and many more). What belief do you think should guide your choices in every area of your life?

For example, here are some life purpose statements:

■ *"My purpose is to love my family and friends."*

■ *"My purpose is to be deeply involved in music."*

■ *"My purpose is stay alive and healthy."*

■ *"My purpose is to learn everything life has to teach me."*

■ *"My purpose is to stay sober and work really hard."*

■ *"My purpose is to keep moving in the right direction."*

Why have a life purpose statement? People who live a purposeful life *get their business handled*. They don't get lost. They make powerful things happen. Just consider what these purposeful students have accomplished:

The purpose of life is a life of purpose.
—Robert Byrne

■ Students at McClintock High School in Arizona donated their hair to an organization named Locks of Love. The organization helps out kids who have lost their own hair because of cancer.

■ Locust Grove Middle School in Georgia donated new baby blankets for infants to the hospital's neonatal intensive care unit. The donations keep babies warm and help out struggling parents, who are coping with their infants' hospitalization, since they can take the blankets home.

Service is the rent we pay to be living. It is the very purpose of life.
—Marian Wright Edelman

■ In New York, students at Oswego High School gave blood at a local donation center to help accident victims and patients who needed surgeries.

■ At Williston High School in North Dakota, students made and donated duffel bags and backpacks to children who had been removed from their homes by Social Services.

■ In Minnesota, Anoka High School students raised money to pay for chemotherapy (cancer treatment) for 12 patients at St. Jude Children's Research Hospital.

■ Students at the Suzanne Middle School in Walnut, California collected Halloween candy, bagged it in 5,000 bags (more than 1,000 pounds of candy) and donated it for a Thanksgiving event at the Los Angeles Mission.

If all the students in the examples on the opposite page shared one purpose, what do you think it would be?

....

....

These students took action because they had a clear purpose. Your purpose should be something that's:

❶ BIG ENOUGH to include all that you want in life.

> *I want to be the best that I can be in everything that I try in life.*

❷ SPECIFIC ENOUGH to explain what you are doing here on this planet.

> *My purpose is to learn as much as I can and share this learning.*

If you don't know what to choose for a life purpose, then just invent a purpose for now. You can change it later. In fact, you can change it any time you wish. It's a good idea to look back at your purpose every year and see if it still fits your life. It's also a good idea to decide if you are still following your life purpose. Please write one sentence below that clearly states the purpose of your life.

My Life Purpose is...

....

....

....

It's alright to not know your life purpose yet. Keep thinking about it. Come back to write it later.

Here is a test to find whether your mission in life is finished: if you are alive, it isn't.
—*Richard Bach*

Choose a Good Road

 If it's true that your life is in your hands, how do you make good choices? There are many ways to go. How do you choose a good road?

First, start with a problem. Any problem. Got a problem? Most of us have lots of problems. Don't have a problem with having a problem. Just pick one and write it down (like I can't stand it when my dad gets so mad at me for nothing, or my lab partner talks way too much, or I don't think I have any friends at this school).

My Problem:

....

....

....

Learn the Four Steps to Success

❶ What's The Problem?

❷ What Do I Want?

❸ What are Three Options?

❹ What's the Best Option? Take Action Right Away.

Four Steps to Success

Use the Four Steps to Success to solve the problem.

❶ What's The Problem?

I don't like my math class. My grades are lousy, my friends keep talking to me so I can't concentrate and I have skipped 5 classes.

❷ What Do I Want?

I want to pass the class, stop skipping classes, and pay attention so I can learn and pass the tests.

❸ What Are Three Options?

I could:

1. try to get in another math class

2. talk to the math teacher; or

3. start doing the homework and sit away from my friends.

❹ What's The Best Option? Take Action Right Away.

I'm going to start doing the homework and sit away from my friends. I'll start homework tonight and sit somewhere else tomorrow. If this doesn't work, I'll try another option.

One may walk over the highest mountain one step at a time.
—John Wanamaker

The first step towards getting somewhere is to decide that you are not going to stay where you are.
—John Pierpont Morgan

Now try the Four Steps to Success to solve one of your problems.

1 What's The Problem?

....

....

2 What Do I Want?

....

....

3 What Are Three Options?

....

....

....

4 What's The Best Option? Take Action Right Away.

Best Option:

....

....

First Action Step:

....

....

The elevator to success is out of order. You'll have to use the stairs... one step at a time.
—Joe Girard

The journey of a thousand miles must begin with a single step.
—Lao Tzu

MAGA AND KEYA ON A GOOD ROAD

Three Learning Skills

As an **ACTIVE LEARNER**, you learn well when you take a leadership role in your learning, for example:

- testing out an idea to see what happens

- going through one step after another on your own

- sharing your ideas with someone else

- jumping right in to begin a project or activity

- taking responsibility for asking questions

As an **INNOVATIVE LEARNER**, you learn well when you try something new and creative, for example:

- offering new ideas that nobody else has raised

- proposing new methods to solving a problem

- putting two ideas together to create something new

- seeing the big picture to understand how ideas fit together

- working well on more than one project at a time

As a **REFLECTIVE LEARNER**, you learn well when you take time to reflect, for example:

- taking time by yourself to think

- stopping after an activity to record your ideas

- journaling about your experiences

- appreciating quiet and focused activities

- pausing to plan before moving on to the next activity

Three Learning Skills: Active, Innovative and Reflective

Review the three learning skills on the opposite page. Students can learn new ideas and skills in many different ways. If you understand that you have many options and learning strategies, you can use more strategies to be a better learner.

A Number the three skills as follows: 1) the skill I prefer to use most often, 2) the skill I prefer to use sometimes, and 3) the skill I prefer to use least often.

1 ....

2 ....

3 ....

B Write down an example of how you have used one of the strategies from the skill you chose as #1 . For instance, if you chose Active Learner, an example might be: I offered to be in charge of creating the PowerPoint for our math team project.

....

....

....

C Write down one way you could use one of the strategies from the skill you chose as #3. For instance, if you chose Innovative Learner, an example might be: I could create a concept map that shows how geometry and social science are connected.

....

....

....

> I'm going to college. I don't care if it ruins my career. I'd rather be smart than a movie star.
> –Natalie Portman

I've taught students in my college classes who had no idea why they were in college: *"I guess I needed something to do after high school,"* one told me. Another one shared, *"I really don't know what I'm doing here. Everyone just told me I should go to college."*

Students who don't know why they're in college often don't do well. Because they don't know how college relates to their life purpose, and because they have no clear goals, they lose motivation. When they lose motivation, they give up when they face a challenge. Since graduating from college is mostly about facing challenges and figuring out how to get past them, it's really hard to succeed when you keep giving up.

You might already know that you want to go to college, or you might not even have thought about it. When the time comes to choose whether or not you want to go to college, you want to be sure you are ready for college. You'll also need to know why college is important to you.

Below are some reasons other students have come up with for attending college:

- I want to go to college so I can get a better job.

- I want to go to college because it will be interesting to learn more.

- I want to go to college because I will get paid more if I have a college degree.

- I want to go to college because lots of my friends will be there too.

- I want to go to college because it will be nice to have more freedom.

Now come up with 3 of your own reasons.

I want to go to college because...

❶ ....
....
....

❷ ....
....
....

❸ ....
....
....

> All the evidence we have is that going to college and earning a bachelor's degree pays off — it's one of the best investments a person can make.
> —Wall Street Journal

> College graduates are more likely to volunteer, vote, and exercise.
> —"Education Pays" Report

Key College Questions

What would I do if I graduated from college?

....

....

....

What contributions could I make to my family and community?

....

....

....

How would it change my life if I went to college?

....

....

....

If I were to go, what would I be willing to do to make it through college?

....

....

....

Flexibility and Adaptability

When I was in high school, I worked for a tree service company. On Saturday mornings we would show up at 8:30 a.m. at the yard, sharpen the chainsaws, load the truck and chop wood until the boss was ready to leave. One morning he told us he needed us to be at work at 8 a.m. starting the next week. The next Saturday I went to work at 8 a.m. At 8:30, as we were just driving away, one of my coworkers drove into the yard. The boss asked him why he was late, and he said: "I've always come at 8:30. That's what I'm used to." "If you can't make it to work at 8 a.m., you can't work here," said my boss, as we drove past, leaving my former coworker there in the driveway.

When the rules of life change, it's no use trying to play by the old rules (not if you want to win the game, at least). Employers report that flexibility and adaptability are crucial skills for effective employees. Technology is always changing; new clients have different needs. A smart business must change its approach as the world changes, and this means that employees must be ready to make changes, some small and some big.

> "
>
> As any jazz musician knows, it takes flexibility and adaptability for improvisation to create beauty.
> —Henry Chesbrough
>
> "

> "
>
> Be firm on principle but flexible on method.
> —Zig Ziglar
>
> "

Practice Flexibility and Adaptability

1 Identify something in your life that hasn't been working (maybe you're not getting to your 3rd period class on time, you're not doing well in geometry, or you're arguing with your sister every night about whose turn it is to set the table). Where are you STUCK?

....

....

....

2 Write down one NEW solution you could try out to change the situation (For example, I could grab my 3rd period textbook from my locker before 1st period, or I could go to the math study hall for 30 minutes after school, or I could ask my sister to agree that we each set the table for two weeks of every month). Where are you willing to bend a little bit?

New Solution:

....

....

....

Growth Mindset

What's the Point?

Write down 2 main points from this chapter (here or in your Road Log).

1 ....
....
....

2 ....

....
....

Create Your Road Log

Please record your learning and ideas in your Road Log.

If someone asked you to explain the 4 Steps To Success,
write down how you would respond.

ideas *in action*

Maria was struggling in high school. Her last three grades on her biology quizzes were all D's.

She thought it was her teacher's fault, Ms. Nuñez. The teacher didn't turn Maria's last two quizzes back before the next quiz, and when she got them back, the quizzes didn't have any comments on them at all, only a big fat D grade. In class it was hard for her to pay attention because Ms. Nuñez spoke so quickly and besides, it was way too hard to understand cell membranes and mitosis. She tried to ask a question once, and Ms. Nuñez completely ignored her. Maria had quit doing her biology homework and barely studied for the tests.

Maria's dad, Mr. Ramirez, didn't know what to do with Maria. He had tried to help her with her homework, but Maria either yelled at him or sat with her arms folded, refusing to talk. Mr. Ramirez told Maria that she couldn't go out with her friends the last three weekends because she wasn't doing well at school. He had met with Ms. Nuñez once, but all she said was, "Maria needs to try harder if she wants to pass the class."

In your opinion, who is most responsible for Maria's problems in school? Who is least responsible? Why?

Ms. Nuñez   Maria   Mr. Ramirez

Most responsible (why?):

....

Least responsible (why?):

....

What were some choices Maria made that led to these problems?

1 ....

2 ....

What different choices could Maria have made to avoid the problems?

1 ....

2 ....

If Maria asked you what she should do, what would you suggest?

1 ....

....

2 ....

....

3 ....

....

Rarely have I made choices that made me feel I was really compromising what I believe.

—Danny Glover

Listen to *Aftermath* by ADAM LAMBERT. Go online to view the song lyrics or listen to the song on YouTube, Grooveshark or another website with video or audio clips. Answer these questions:

What does Lambert say about getting lost in your life?

....

....

....

Write down one of the points of this chapter and choose a line from the song that is related to this point.

POINT

....

....

LINE

....

....

....

What did you learn?

I know you've learned a few important things!

....

....

....

....

....

....

....

....

....

....

....

....

....

....

People take different roads seeking fulfillment and happiness. Just because they're not on your road doesn't mean they've gotten lost.

—H. Jackson Brown, Jr.

NEVER GIVE UP!!!

 Remember Your Life Purpose

The defense of our rights and our dignity, as well as efforts never to let ourselves to be overcome by the feeling of hatred–this is the road we have chosen.

—Lech Walesa

Research suggests that people with a life purpose are happier and more effective.

PEOPLE WHO HAVE NO CLEAR LIFE PURPOSE:

■ Rarely think about the future and what to contribute or achieve

■ Have trouble making effective decisions and can wander aimlessly

■ Lack motivation or the desire to take action

PEOPLE WHO HAVE A CLEAR LIFE PURPOSE:

■ Have goals and a strong sense of direction

■ Feel that their lives have meaning

■ Use values that guide their decisions

■ Create a positive life experience for themselves

Write Your Life Purpose here and then on an index card and post it where you'll see it (review page 39). Use big bold letters to make sure you remember it:

CHAPTER THREE
DREAMING BIG

Read the chapter to answer these preview questions.

How do you know when you're walking a good road?

Why do you need to set goals?

What are your most important values?

Do you learn best by yourself or with others?

Who is Duane De Witt and what can you learn from him?

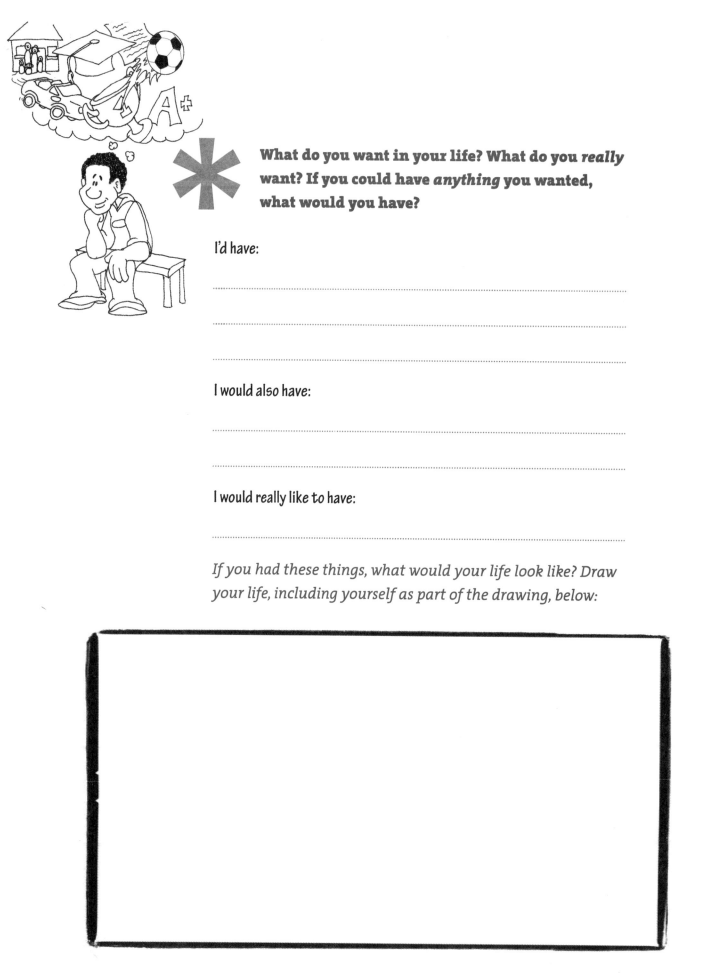

What do you want in your life? What do you *really* want? If you could have *anything* you wanted, what would you have?

I'd have:

....

....

....

I would also have:

....

....

I would really like to have:

....

If you had these things, what would your life look like? Draw your life, including yourself as part of the drawing, below:

If you really could *have* anything you wanted, what might you *give away to other people*?

I'd *give* away:

....

I'd also give away:

....

I would really like to give away:

....

If you could *do* anything you wanted (fly to any country, run faster than anyone on earth, make a music video, visit someone you miss), what would you *do*?

I would:

....

I would also:

....

I would be sure to:

....

If you could *be* any way you wish (happy, peaceful, powerful, funny), how would you *be*?

I would be:

....

I would also be:

....

I think I could be:

....

When goal goes, meaning goes; when meaning goes, purpose goes; when purpose goes, life goes dead on our hands.
—Carl Jung

Choosing a Good Road

There are many roads, many paths to choose from in your life. In the ancient Lakota Indian story, PtesanWi (White Buffalo Calf Woman) announces that she will bring special gifts to the Lakota people. They prepare a medicine lodge, a ritual healing site, for her visit. She arrives with a mysterious bundle. In the bundle is a sacred Lakota object, representing all peoples, everything that grows and the wind that carries prayers to the Great Spirit, Wakan Tanka. She teaches the Lakota people Seven Sacred Rituals, and that they must remember the lessons she taught them so they will follow the good red road. The good red road is the life path that leads them in the right direction.

Oh hear me grandfathers, and help us, that our generation in the future will live and walk the good road with the flowering stick to success.

—Black Elk & John Niehardt

How do you choose a road that will lead you in the right direction? In the Four Steps activity in Chapter Two, you were asked to choose the Best Option and Take Action Right Away. But how do you know what the Best Option is?

GOALS & ACTION STEPS

To help you choose the best option, you should be clear about your goals. Goals are the stepping stones on the road to your bigger dreams. Action Steps move you forward to help reach your goals.

It's hard to decide which road to choose if you don't know where you're going. Goals will allow us to decide where we want to go, and then we can keep checking the map to see if we're heading in the right direction. Got **BIG DREAMS**? Set goals that take you there.

Dreams

What are some of your life dreams? For example: *My dream is to open my own restaurant; my dream is to start an organization that feeds hungry people; my dream is to have all my family members living together without any fighting.*

YOUR DREAMS:

A ....

....

....

....

What kinda dream is this?
—Beyoncé Knowles

B ....

....

....

....

C ....

....

....

The fool wanders; the wise man travels.
—Thomas Fuller

 Now take one of these dreams and draw it on the next page. Draw what would it look like if you were right in the middle of your dream (draw yourself in there, too).

My Dream

Create Your Road Log

Please record your learning and ideas in your Road Log.

If someone asked you to explain one of your life dreams,
write down how you would respond.

What's the Point?

Write down 2 main points from this chapter (here or in your Road Log).

1 ....

....

....

2 ....

....

....

Once you get clear on your dreams and purpose, you can identify several **VALUES** that will help keep you on the right path. For example, *I value honesty, friendship, and careful listening.* What do you value?

If we are to go forward, we must go back and rediscover those precious values.
—Martin Luther King, Jr.

The aim of education is the knowledge, not of facts, but of values.
—William S. Burroughs

I value:

....

I value:

....

I value:

....

Our problem is not to find better values but to be faithful to those we profess.
—John W. Gardner

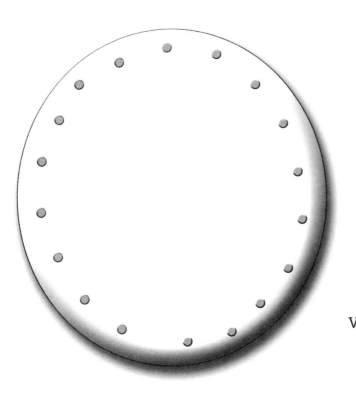

Choose one value that you believe will protect you from life's many challenges. If you were to consistently follow this value, you'd feel confident that you'd be choosing a good road. Write the name of the value in the center of the Value Shield.

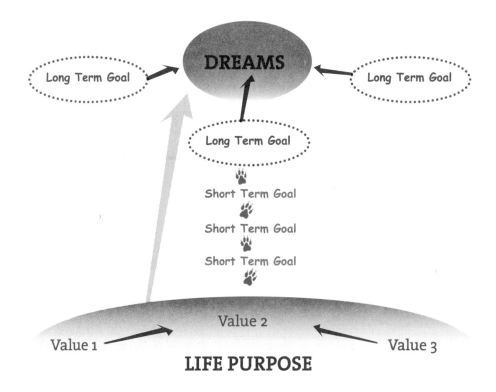

Put It All Together

Your **LIFE PURPOSE** is directed by your **VALUES**. You use **ACTION STEPS** to reach **SHORT TERM GOALS**. Eventually you reach **LONG TERM GOALS**. Keep moving forward and finally you achieve an important **DREAM**.

Setting Goals: D.R.E.A.M.

Setting and reaching goals allows us to achieve our dreams. When you set goals, try using the **D.R.E.A.M.** model:

Detailed

Realistic

Energetic

Affirmative

Mine

DETAILED with a **timeline**: It is easier to be certain that we have accomplished a goal when it is **detailed**, focused and has a **timeline**. "I want to get better at writing" is general and unscheduled, not detailed. The following revised goal is detailed: "I intend to learn the rules for the 5 most frequent grammar errors and reduce these errors in my next essay by at least 2 errors per page, within the next 6 weeks."

REALISTIC: Be certain that your goal is attainable, but you should stretch your imagination. You don't need to know exactly what actions you'll take to achieve your goal. Yet be careful to stay **realistic** about what is possible for you to achieve. Unrealistic goals are nearly impossible to accomplish and not reaching goals might lead us to give up on achieving our dreams.

ENERGETIC: Got zing? If you're bored (or yawn) when reading your own goals, perhaps you might rethink them. Maybe the dream is not powerful enough. Perhaps the goals you outlined are not closely related to reaching your dream. Maybe you're ready for a new or bigger challenge. Be certain that your goals are **energetic**, invested with excitement and energy.

AFFIRMATIVE: Check your goal to see that it is moving you in an **affirmative** direction. Some goals are negative: "I don't want to eat junk food." They can be written instead in an affirmative style to keep you focused on what you do want: "I want to eat at least three servings of fruit every day for the next month."

MINE: It is often a major challenge to stay motivated to achieve someone else's dream. Sometimes we take on dreams that belong to others, perhaps to family or friends. Be certain that this dream is real and compelling to you, compelling enough to carry you through many years of hard work to accomplish it. This is *your* goal!

Dream on . . .

Dream on . . .

Dream on . . .

Dream until your

dreams come true.

—Aerosmith

Try setting goals for one of your high school classes, then revising them. For example:

DETAILED with a **timeline**: *I want to have an A average in my US History class by next week.*

Revise for Realistic: Example: *Well, I guess it might take longer than one week to turn my grades around. Since I haven't earned an A on any test or assignment in 7 weeks, maybe I need to be more realistic.*

REALISTIC: *I want to earn at least a B+ average in my US History class tests within 4 weeks and not fail any of the quizzes.*

Revise for Energetic: Example: *I'd like to get a B+ but I'm not that excited about just the grade. I am very engaged in my group project since that's fun and really interesting.*

ENERGETIC: *I want to earn at least a B+ on my March 5th upcoming history group project and not fail any of the quizzes.*

Revise for Affirmative: Example: *I guess "not fail any of the quizzes" is not an affirmative goal. I'll try revising this part to make it what I actually want to happen.*

AFFIRMATIVE: *I want to earn at least a B+ on my March 5th upcoming history group project and get at least a C+ on all the quizzes.*

Revise for Mine: Example: *I think what I really care about is doing a great job on the PowerPoint for my group project since that's my part of the project.*

MINE: *I want to earn at least a B+ on my March 5th upcoming history group project, create a very cool PowerPoint, and get at least a C+ on all the quizzes.*

The tragedy of life doesn't lie in not reaching your goal. The tragedy lies in having no goals to reach.

—Benjamin Mays

YOUR TURN! Set a goal for one of your classes and revise it, using the D.R.E.A.M. approach.

DETAILED with a timeline: *I want . . .*

....

....

....

....

Revise for Realistic:

....

....

....

....

REALISTIC: *I want . . .*

....

....

....

....

Revise for Energetic:

....

....

....

....

One day I had a dream
I tried to chase it
But I wasn't going
nowhere, running man!
—*Tinie Tempah*

ENERGETIC: *I want . . .*

....

....

....

....

Revise for Affirmative:

....

....

....

AFFIRMATIVE: *I want . . .*

....

....

....

....

Revise for Mine:

....

....

....

MINE: *I want . . .*

....

....

....

First build a proper goal. That proper goal will make it easy, almost automatic, to build a proper You.

—Johann von Goethe

Peace is not merely a distant goal that we seek, but a means by which we arrive at that goal.

— Martin Luther King, Jr.

A Dream Deferred

The poet Langston Hughes wondered what happens when we quit dreaming, or when we can't reach our dreams, or put them off without achieving them. Do the dreams "dry up like a raisin"...or rot away...collapse...or maybe "explode?" Dreams that are put off, or that are not reached, are dreams deferred. What do you think happens to a dream deferred?

A Dream Deferred

CREATE A CARTOON

In the three panels above, create your own cartoon that represents the title: A DREAM DEFERRED. Maybe it's one character with clouds showing his/her thoughts or words. Maybe it's two characters having a conversation. Your choice, of course.

Three Learning Skills

As a SOLO LEARNER, you learn well when you can work by yourself and focus, for example:

- being in charge of your own project

- studying alone for a test

- completing an in-class activity without help

- being energized by a quiet environment where you can reflect

- reviewing and revising your own work

As a PAIRING LEARNER, you learn well when partnering with one other person, for example:

- trying new ideas out with another person

- listening carefully to each other

- studying for a test with one other person

- partnering up on a lab assignment

- paying attention with focused energy to only one other set of ideas

As a GROUP LEARNER, you learn well when engaging with multiple learners, for example:

- leading a group through a project

- hearing a lot of different ideas

- being in the middle of a loud group

- staying focused with high energy in the classroom

- being inspired by multiple ideas and the presence of other students

Three Learning Skills: Solo, Pairing and Group

Review the three learning skills on the opposite page. Students can learn new ideas and skills in many different ways. If you understand that you have many options and learning strategies, you can use more strategies to be a better learner.

A Number the three skills as follows: 1) the skill I prefer to use most often, 2) the skill I prefer to use sometimes, and 3) the skill I prefer to use least often.

1 ....

2 ....

3 ....

B Write down an example of how you have used one of the strategies from the skill you chose as #1. For instance, if you chose Pairing Learner, an example might be: I partnered up on a biology lab assignment.

....

....

....

C Write down one way you could use one of the strategies from the skill you chose as #3. For instance, if you chose Solo Learner, an example might be: I could go to the library by myself, find a quiet corner and review for my Spanish test.

....

....

....

Ready for College

If you don't dream big, you'll live small. If college is not part of your vision, it might not happen. What you expect from yourself is usually what you get.

What others expect from you may also be what you get. It turns out that if your teachers don't believe in your ability to make it to college, it will make it harder for you to get there. They may lower their expectations for you. It doesn't mean that anyone can stop you from making it into college, but you will need to speak up for yourself if you really want it. Here's what to try:

① Get clear on what's important to you about college.

Go back to your answers to Key College Questions in Ready for College in Chapter Two (page 48). What?! You didn't answer those yet? It's not too late–go ahead and do it now before coming back to this page.

② Tell someone your reasons for wanting to go to college.

Make it happen. Today, or before the end of the next school day, make an appointment with a college advisor, guidance counselor, or one of your favorite teachers to talk about your dreams and hopes for college. Seek out one or two elders you respect in your family or community. Ask if you could share your ideas with them, and ask for their help in making it happen. Go with a friend if you want. Most teachers or elders would love to hear what you think is important, and would love to help you get what you want.

ADVISOR, COUNSELOR, TEACHER OR ELDER'S NAME:

....

DAY AND TIME OF YOUR APPOINTMENT OR MEETING:

....

③ Show them by your choices that you mean what you say.

Now this is where you show them you're serious about getting what you want. If you tell them you want to go to college but don't even show up to math class, you're not walking your talk. That's why choices are so important. Practice making choices that keep you on a good road for the next week. Show them, and show yourself, that you really want this. Walk your talk.

The Spanish word *"palabra"* means *"word"* in English. But when someone asks you in Spanish, *"Palabra?"*, it means, "Are you giving me your promise that you will follow through on what you said?" When you answer, *"Palabra,"* it means, "I promise. You have my word." Give your promise that you will do what you say. It will make a big difference in your life if you do so. *Palabra.*

④ Ask them to give you a challenge and then step up.

It turns out that taking challenging classes in high school is really important for getting into college. Ask for a schedule of classes that will prepare you to go to college. Once you're closer to graduating, you can choose your next steps. If you haven't completed the important classes, it won't be as easy to choose the road to college.

What's the Point?

Write down 2 main points from this chapter (here or in your Road Log).

1 ....
....
....

2 ....

....
....

Create Your Road Log

Please record your learning and ideas in your Road Log.

If someone asked you to explain the word "Palabra,"
write down how you would respond.

Entrepreneurial Skills

An entrepreneur is someone who sees a problem and has the drive to seek a solution. They often start small businesses that may grow to be very large. They are innovators in their field. There are entrepreneurs in the business world and also social or global entrepreneurs with goals to create social change, like getting millions of people to recycle their glass bottles. Here are four skills that most entrepreneurs have (or need to learn):

1 Vision: They see opportunities for improvement in the world.

2 Drive and Persistence: They are very self-motivated and enthusiastic.

3 Commitment: They don't stop trying until they have reached their goal.

4 Resilience: Entrepreneurs often make mistakes because they are taking risks, and thus they fail many times before succeeding. They have resilience, the ability to bounce back from a failure, to pick themselves up, and to keep going.

Give yourself a score, from 1 (still much to learn) to 10 (great at this) in each area:

_____ Vision

_____ Drive and Persistence

_____ Commitment

_____ Resilience

Pick one entrepreneurial skill to work on for the next three weeks and return here to score yourself:

Week One Score _____

Week Two Score _____

Week Three Score _____

Pay attention to how you use this skill. Do you sometimes quit trying, or lose drive when you feel bored? Where are you improving? For example, perhaps you are getting better at seeing "opportunities for improvement in the world." If you'd like to be an entrepreneur in the future, practice these skills now. You might want to start your own entrepreneurial project now and put your skills to use.

Where do you think the world (or your community) needs your talents in making improvements?

....

....

....

> " I have been sustained by three saving graces — my family, my friends, and a faith in the power of resilience and hope.
> —Elizabeth Edwards

ideas in action

Duane De Witt was the speaker at a University of California, Berkeley graduation. In his short speech, he asked that other graduates help disadvantaged Californians get into a university and graduate. This 48-year-old Army vet had to move past many of his own obstacles to graduate.

Action conquers fear.
—Peter Nivio Zarlenga

His application had been rejected four years in a row. He still kept taking classes at a junior college. He spent seven hours (three times a week) on a bus to come to UC Berkeley and take only one class. He finally showed up to a meeting of university college board members and had one minute to make his case. They admitted him.

He often drove to visit his mentally ill mother, who was unable to keep him as a child. He was homeless and slept in the woods on the campus, washing up in the restroom each morning. He once lost everything when someone broke into his old Subaru station wagon, stealing his textbooks, class notes, tools, sleeping bag and clothing.

But De Witt would not give up. He told himself that this was his last opportunity. As he continued on the way to his dream of graduating from college, he also realized he had a new life purpose: to help poor people get decent and affordable housing. He helped save a senior citizen mobile home park in his hometown. He entered a graduate program to learn more. He knew what he wanted to achieve and he wouldn't give up. Period.

1 If you were talking with Duane, and told him you weren't sure you could graduate from college, what do you think he would tell you? Write down some of it here:

....

....

....

2 Think of a line or some words from a song you know that Duane might have as his favorite song because they explain his attitude about life. Write down the song title, artist and some lines here:

....

....

....

....

3 Make up a quote from an interview with De Witt, in which he explains in one sentence how he was able to succeed:

....

....

....

Listen to *Never Give Up* by YOLANDA ADAMS. Look up the lyrics online. Write down two lines that are most motivating to you and explain why:

What did you learn?

I know you've learned a few important things!

_____

_____

_____

_____

_____

_____

_____

_____

_____

_____

_____

_____

" *Your goals are the road maps that guide you and show you what is possible for your life.* **"**

—Les Brown

NEVER GIVE UP!!!

 **Focus on the Goal**

People who pay attention to their goals are more likely to keep going until they accomplish them. If you feel like giving up, or just stop caring about whether you are a success, here's what you need to know:

1 People who write down their goals are more likely to achieve them. Write down one of your most important goals.

MY IMPORTANT GOAL:

....

2 People who also share their written goals and intended actions with someone else are more likely to achieve them. Identify a contact: friend, family member, mentor or teacher. Share your important goal and your commitment to taking action to reach it.

Who will you call, text, IM, email, write to, or visit?

....

3 People who share written goals and actions and also send a weekly update are the most likely to achieve them. How often (daily, weekly, every month) will you update your contact on your progress in reaching your goal?

HOW OFTEN?

....

If we know where we want to go, then even a stony road is bearable.
—Horst Hoehler

Goals are not only absolutely necessary to motivate us. They are essential to really keep us alive.
—Robert H. Schuller

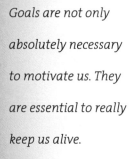

Cool Facts

- People who write down their goals achieve over 50% more of their goals than those who do not write them down.

- Goal setting is very important for high school athletes. Establishing goals helps athletes to work harder, and results in higher motivation levels. As their motivation increases, their athletic performance also increases.

- Bono, a founder of the group U2, says: "My goal, my job, is to put myself out of a job. So I can be in a rock band in all good conscience." His goal led him to form, along with members of Green Day, Alicia Keyes and Bill Gates, the ONE campaign (ONE.org). They have recruited more than 2.5 million members to help them fight extreme poverty and disease in Africa.

    As a result, nearly 4 million Africans have access to life-saving AIDS medication, and Malaria deaths have been cut in half in countries across Africa. 42 million more children are now going to school. Their new goal: a new childhood vaccines campaign to help save 4 million kids' lives in 5 years.

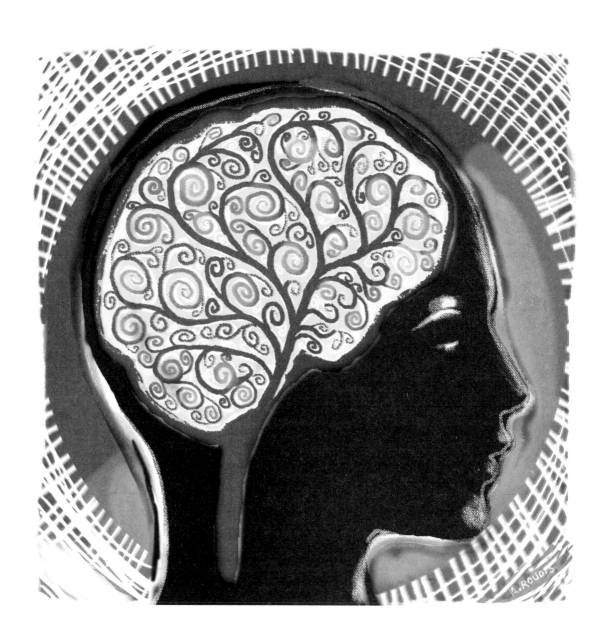

CHAPTER FOUR

GETTING SMARTER = WORKING HARDER

Read the chapter to answer these preview questions.

What are the different ways people can be intelligent?

What is an important area for you to grow in your life?

Which of the Nine Learner Types are you?

How do you know when someone is an Adapting Learner?

What is the difference between a Fixed Mindset and a Growth Mindset?

Getting Smarter = Working Harder

Have you ever felt like you weren't very smart? I sure have. Have you ever been in a classroom where you were confused, but some of the other students seemed to understand the lesson? Have you studied hard or participated in class activities, but still struggled or felt like you didn't *really* understand? The problem might be that you need to learn more about how you learn best.

Many talented people have struggled in school. They had extraordinary talents that were overlooked by others, and sometimes they even overlooked their own talents.

- Cartoonist Charles Schultz, whose Peanuts comic strip (featuring Snoopy) is world famous, didn't appear to be talented in high school. Every cartoon he submitted was rejected by the editor of his high school yearbook.

- Althea Gibson was the first African American woman to win the Wimbledon tennis tournament, and she followed up by winning the US Open. Yet Gibson is said to have struggled when she was in school.

- Albert Einstein, the Nobel Prize-winning scientist, wasn't considered smart when he was a young student in school.

Of course these gifted experts in their fields were intelligent. The truth is there are many ways to be intelligent. Having learned about myelin, you know that working hard is the key to becoming smarter. However, hard work is not enough. You also need to work *smarter*, paying attention to the different ways students learn.

Some students prefer to study alone, while others do better in a group. Some students like to be leaders in classroom conversations, while others contribute and learn best behind the scenes. Some students highly value making their assignments original and creative while others value making sure they have carefully followed directions.

Some students also face learning disabilities that add an extra layer of challenge to their learning process. They need to use additional learning strategies. For these students, asking for help to learn these strategies is crucial.

Struggling with learning doesn't mean you're not intelligent. It just means that you're struggling. The more you understand about the many ways you are intelligent, the better you'll be able to put your intelligences to work.

NINE TYPES OF LEARNERS

This chapter introduces nine different types of learners in the next section. Nobody is limited to one type of learning. We all have the ability to learn through any of these learner types. It's true that we often have preferences for how we like to learn. We also have habits of learning, strategies that we have been using for many years. It is important to understand our preferences and habits of learning. It is also important to stretch ourselves to try new ways of learning too.

The Nine Learners

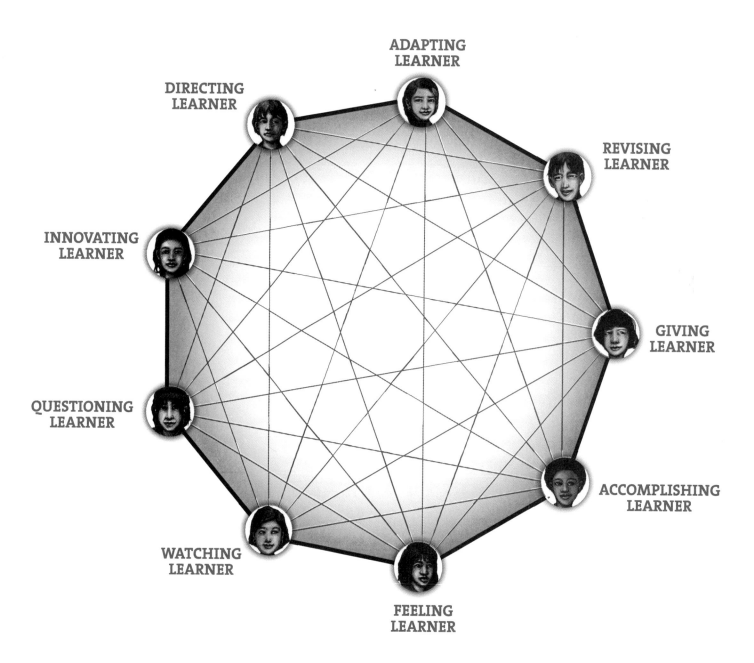

ADAPTING
LEARNER

DIRECTING
LEARNER

REVISING
LEARNER

INNOVATING
LEARNER

GIVING
LEARNER

QUESTIONING
LEARNER

ACCOMPLISHING
LEARNER

WATCHING
LEARNER

FEELING
LEARNER

Nine Learning Strengths

REVISING LEARNER Good at spotting mistakes. Likes everything to be just right. Organized, orderly and meets deadlines. Follows rules carefully. Likes to teach others. Often very practical. Likes to be thorough and precise. Sees importance of values and ideals. Considers consequences of actions.

GIVING LEARNER Knows other students' needs. Contributes and likes to feel needed. Remembers what others have done. Works behind the scenes. Likes emotional connection to assignments. Pays attention to audience and seeks approval.

ACCOMPLISHING LEARNER Wants to score high on tests and homework. Likes to compete and win. Very adaptable to changes. Ambitious in taking on challenges. Motivated to perform. Confident in abilities.

FEELING LEARNER Wants to make assignments original and creative. Shares strong feelings about ideas. Sees what is missing from others' ideas/projects. Very aware of himself as a learner. Encourages others to go beyond the basics. Good at seeing the deeper importance of ideas.

WATCHING LEARNER Good at careful observations and testing ideas. Has organized and logical approach to learning. Thoughtful, curious and focused learner. Can see existing patterns easily. Independent and innovative learner. Often very thorough. Dives deeply into one subject. Visionary and intensive thinker.

QUESTIONING LEARNER Can ask tough questions. Challenges others to rethink their positions. Can be relied on to do what they say. Hardworking with strong commitment. Likes to know and follow the rules and directions. Easily spots conflicting ideas. Supports others whose ideas may be ignored.

 INNOVATING LEARNER Likes to create new ideas. Sees the big picture. Enthusiastically takes on many projects. Understands new perspectives. Quickly absorbs new information and skills. Puts together creative approaches and leads others. Productive, spontaneous and has a positive attitude. Good at planning.

 DIRECTING LEARNER Good at leading others. Confident of ability to get assignments done. Certain of what to do. Speaks up for the unprotected. Calls it like it is. Resourceful and independent. Persists until the work is finished. Clear on opinions and ideas.

 ADAPTING LEARNER Flexible in approach. Appreciates all students' ideas and opinions. Can mediate and solve conflicts. Easy to get along with. Good at finding a simple solution. Imaginative and strongly visual. Patient in solving problems. Works steadily and persistently. Sees all parts of an issue. Accepting of contradiction and complexity.

Growth Mindset

Reviewing Nine Learner Strengths

Your biology teacher asks students to work in groups to prepare for a test, reviewing textbook pages on cells.

Learning is not compulsory... neither is survival.
—W. Edwards Deming

How would a **REVISING LEARNER** respond to this assignment? For example, he might organize the group and ask everyone to review 2 pages. A Revising Learner might also...

....

....

....

How would a **GIVING LEARNER** respond to this assignment? For example, he might remember that one student had done well on an earlier test on cells and ask her to explain cell division to the group. A Giving Learner might also...

....

....

....

How would an **ACCOMPLISHING LEARNER** respond to this assignment? For example, she might want to compete with students in other groups, trying to finish the review first. An Accomplishing Learner might also...

....

....

....

Your geometry teacher asks students to go up to the board and calculate angles in a triangle.

How would a **FEELING LEARNER** respond to this assignment? A Feeling Learner might...

....

....

....

How would a **WATCHING LEARNER** respond to this assignment? A Watching Learner might...

....

....

....

How would a **QUESTIONING LEARNER** respond to this assignment? A Questioning Learner might...

....

....

....

Taking charge of your own learning is a part of taking charge of your life.

—Warren G. Bennis

Your PE teacher asks students to go to the field, form two teams and play a new game using two soccer balls, lacrosse sticks, but keeping their hands behind their backs.

How would an **INNOVATING LEARNER** respond to this assignment? An Innovating Learner might...

....

....

....

How would a **DIRECTING LEARNER** respond to this assignment? A Directing Learner might ...

....

....

....

How would an **ADAPTING LEARNER** respond to this assignment? An Adapting Learner might...

....

....

....

NINE LEARNERS
Opportunities for Learning

REVISING LEARNER Can be obsessive about rules and upset when they are not followed. Can be overly critical of self and others. Can insist on controlled and perfect results. Might be hesitant to try really challenging or completely new activities. Might forget to stop and enjoy learning.

GIVING LEARNER Can lose sight of meeting own needs and ideas. Can be overly concerned with teacher and student feedback. Might be very controlling and demand that others listen to his/her ideas and solutions. Feels hurt when perceiving rejection. Can disrupt others because of a focus on attention and being a part of the group, or popular. Will demand attention when experiencing being disliked.

ACCOMPLISHING LEARNER Can be overly competitive. Will sometimes bend the rules or invent new rules. Might ignore own feelings. Can burn out by doing too much. Can have difficulty staying with something extremely challenging.

To become different from what we are, we must have some awareness of what we are.

—Eric Hoffer

FEELING LEARNER Can be impractical and disorganized in finishing work. Can overvalue feelings and undervalue facts as important in learning. Can dislike the ways things have been done before and not want to be seen as just like others. May not pay great attention to the consequences of decisions. When focused on what's missing, can forget to value what is there. Can create drama and conflict. Might take things personally, and become envious of others.

 WATCHING LEARNER Can get overly focused on just one idea. Can withdraw from group projects. Can avoid feelings and escape from life by retreating into the mind. Might withhold ideas when sensing others do not immediately understand or appear to care. Can become isolated.

 QUESTIONING LEARNER May struggle with anxiety over projects and tests. Can be overly suspicious or pessimistic. Might challenge others too strongly. Can panic under pressure. May challenge teachers as an authority or may surrender under authority and give up. Can become anxious when on stage.

 INNOVATING LEARNER Can be undisciplined and lose focus. May take on too many projects and commitments. May become lost in future planning. Has a hard time accepting critical feedback. Can have trouble sustaining excitement to complete long projects.

 DIRECTING LEARNER Can become bossy and controlling. Often needs to be more sensitive to others' feelings and needs. May become overly confident of ability to get assignments done. Can be opinionated and resist thinking carefully. Sometimes unwilling to see others' ideas or perspectives. May ignore others' roles and become overly independent. Can have trouble accepting feedback.

ADAPTING LEARNER Can fail to take a stand or not know what he/she wants. Might focus too much on trying to prevent problems. Can have hard time in making a final decision and being assertive. Might get carried along by conflicting values of other students. Can procrastinate on completing a project and get distracted by other things.

 Each of us has patterns of behavior. Seeing and understanding these patterns allows us to learn something important about ourselves. Each of the nine types has strengths in learning, but also opportunities to learn and choose new, more effective behaviors. Which of the nine types describes you most accurately, and why?

I am a/an .... **Learner**

Explain why, using some of the words in the learner description. For example, I am sometimes unwilling to see others' ideas.

....

....

....

Now identify an action you could take to choose a new more effective behavior. For example, if you were an **ADAPTING LEARNER,** you might "focus too much on trying to prevent problems." An action you might take to change this behavior would be to "respond to problems by allowing people to disagree and set a new goal."

Action: ....

....

FIXED MINDSET VERSUS GROWTH MINDSET

Researcher Carol Dweck at Stanford University examined student attitudes about intelligence. The key to academic (and other) success, she found, isn't ability. Success depends on whether you look at ability as something you already have or as something that can be developed through effort.

Students with a Fixed Mindset believe that they are as smart as they will ever be. They believe that either you are smart in math, or in writing, or in science, or you're not. They do not see that if you work hard to learn, and if you practice skills, you will become better ("smarter") at those skills.

These students give up easily when faced with a challenge, whether they believe they are "smart" at a subject or "not smart" at a subject. They care more about looking smart than learning something challenging. They won't try anything challenging because they don't want to look like failures.

Students with a Growth Mindset believe that they can become smarter through effort. They know they can work hard to become smarter in math, or writing, or science (or soccer), and eventually will achieve their goals. They have no higher level of IQ, simply a different belief system. Their belief about the value of hard work means they don't give up on learning something difficult. They clearly see the connection between practicing skills and becoming better ("smarter") at those skills. They believe they can become "smarter" through effort and persistence. They prioritize mastering new ideas.

IMPLEMENTATION

Students in one middle school learned to improve their motivation and grades. 50% of the students in the class attended a workshop where they were taught study skills only. The study skills did not have an impact because they did not have the motivation to put them into practice.

50% of the students attended a different workshop that taught them that their brain is like a muscle, and it gets stronger when you use it. Every time you learn something new, you increase your intelligence. Dr. Dweck asked them if they thought babies were dumb. Students laughed and said of course not, they're still learning. The students were taught that they too are still developing their brains. They read an article about how their brains become smarter. They had a lot of discussion about effort and how it leads to improvement.

At the end of the semester, the brain workshop students showed significant improvement in grades and motivation levels. Their teachers didn't know at the time that there were two workshops with different content, but afterwards they could identify the differences in the two groups of students. Students with a Fixed Mindset gave up easily when given something challenging. Students with a Growth Mindset kept trying until they learned a new skill.

Which mindset will you use to accomplish your goals?

Fixed Mindset Students

- believe that they are as smart as they will *ever be* in math, or writing, or science (or soccer).

- give up easily when faced with a challenge.

- believe they are "smart" at a subject or "not smart" at a subject.

- won't try anything challenging because they don't want to look like failures.

When have you had a fixed mindset? About a subject like English, math or PE? About a sport, like basketball, baseball or soccer? About a skill like dancing, or cooking?

Growth Mindset Students

- know they can work hard to become smarter in math, or writing, or science (or soccer).

- don't give up on learning something difficult.

- believe that they can become smarter through effort.

- prioritize learning new ideas, even if they are taking risks.

What's the Point?

Write down 2 main points from this chapter (here or in your Road Log).

1 ....

....

....

2 ....

....

....

Cool Facts

- Students with a Growth Mindset use better learning strategies than students with a Fixed Mindset.

- Students with a Growth Mindset get better grades in math than students with a Fixed Mindset.

- Anyone can learn to change to a Growth Mindset.

- A Fixed Mindset will make you only try easy things in life.

- College students with a Fixed Mindset about handling emotions had more problems managing their emotions during their first year in college.

Create Your Road Log

Please record your learning and ideas in your Road Log.

If someone asked you to explain a "Growth Mindset," write down how you would respond.

Three Learning Skills

As a DETAIL LEARNER, you learn well when you focus on the details of an assignment or activity, for example:

- correcting small problems before moving on

- asking many questions about assignments before beginning

- valuing being organized to capture everything that needs to be done

- needing time to look through the handouts or text

- discussing one small idea or issue for a long time

As a PROCESS LEARNER, you learn well when you focus on each step of an assignment or activity, for example:

- learning through step-by-step directions

- following directions in the order received

- needing to experience a concept and not just hear about it

- valuing taking an active role in the learning process

- asking for more guidance and clearer directions

As a BIG PICTURE LEARNER, you learn well when you focus on the connections between ideas, assignments and activities, for example:

- knowing how an idea is connected to another idea

- moving quickly into a project and exploring many ideas

- understanding the expected goal or outcome

- asking why this activity or assignment is important

- valuing ideas that are shared across different cultures

Three Learning Skills: Detail, Process and Big Picture

Review the three learning skills on the opposite page. Students can learn new ideas and skills in many different ways. If you understand that you have many options and learning strategies, you can use more strategies to be a better learner.

A Number the three skills as follows: 1) the skill I prefer to use most often, 2) the skill I prefer to use sometimes, and 3) the skill I prefer to use least often.

1 ....

2 ....

3 ....

B Write down an example of how you have used one of the strategies from the skill you chose as #1. For instance, if you chose Process Learner, an example might be: I closely followed directions on my U.S. history project.

....

....

....

C Write down one way you could use one of the strategies from the skill you chose as #3. For instance, if you chose Big Picture Learner, an example might be: I could explore more ideas before starting work on my next life skills assignment.

....

....

....

ideas in action

You're a student in a geometry classroom with a brand new high school teacher, Ms. Sarkossian, and it's her first week on the job.

The other students don't seem to care about the class or learning anything. Some come late to class. Some students sit in the very back of the class and talk to each other when Ms. Sarkossian is trying to teach a new idea to the class. When she asked one of the students who was talking if he wanted to learn geometry, he said: "I don't think I can. I've never been able to understand math. I just don't think I was cut out to be a math student."

At the end of class, Ms. Sarkossian asks to speak with you. "I'm out of ideas," she says. "I'm not sure the other students are willing to learn. Maybe they're too scared. Do you have any suggestions?"

Using some of the ideas from this chapter, please advise Ms. Sarkossian on three activities she might try to get students to stop talking and start learning. For example, she might put the students into pairs and ask them to keep working on one problem until they have solved it. Why? This could show them that they can actually do math, if they are willing to keep trying. Now it's your turn.

Recommend three activities Ms. Sarkossian could use that would help her students learn better:

1 ....

....

Why? Explain:

....

....

....

2 ....

....

Why? Explain:

....

....

....

3 ....

....

Why? Explain:

....

....

....

Happiness is not something ready made. It comes from your own actions.
—Dalai Lama

Ready for College

There is one simple fact about college that you need to know: students with strong reading and writing skills graduate more quickly. This does not mean that you won't graduate college if you are not a strong reader and writer. This does mean that reading and writing skills are really important. You can improve your skills if you have a Growth Mindset. Here are four basic strategies to improve your skills:

- Increase your vocabulary by writing new words on flash cards or use a smartphone app. Study until you can use the words correctly.

- Strengthen your reading skills by reading more often. Remember how to build myelin sheath: use Effective Practice!

- Write something every day. Try this in your Road Log.

- Meet with your English teacher and ask for more suggestions.

If English is not your first language, you can still make major improvements in reading and writing English. There are language classes you can take to learn more. Many college students speak a language other than English at home.

If you are a student with reading or writing disabilities (like dyslexia), you too can make major improvements in reading and writing English.

How can you accomplish all this? Ask for help and use a Growth Mindset!

> In college, you learn how to learn. Four years is not too much time to spend at that.
> –Mary Oliver

Creativity & Innovation

"Creativity is inventing, experimenting, growing, taking risks, breaking rules, making mistakes, and having fun."
— *Mary Lou Cook*

When you start your career, you'll find something very familiar: challenges to be solved. Just like at school and at home, you will face many challenges. Many employees spend hours each day just finding solutions to challenges. Employers want their employees to do two things well:

 Come up with new ideas and solutions (Creativity)

2 Put those ideas and solutions into action (Innovation)

Theodore Levitt, a professor at Harvard Business School, wrote, "Creativity is thinking up new things. Innovation is doing new things." Try both. Using the boxes on the opposite page, in the top box, draw a problem. In the bottom, draw the solution. For a problem, you might draw a crowded line of students at the cafeteria. For a solution, you might draw a student eating a tasty lunch from home.

PROBLEM

SOLUTION

Listen to *Work* by DEPECHE MODE. Look up the lyrics online. The song includes the following lyrics: "You got to work hard" and "Nothing comes easy." Do you agree or disagree with this idea? Write your thoughts below, as a short paragraph or as a song lyric of your own:

You got to work hard...

....

....

....

....

Nothing comes easy...

....

....

....

....

What did you learn?

I know you've learned a few important things!

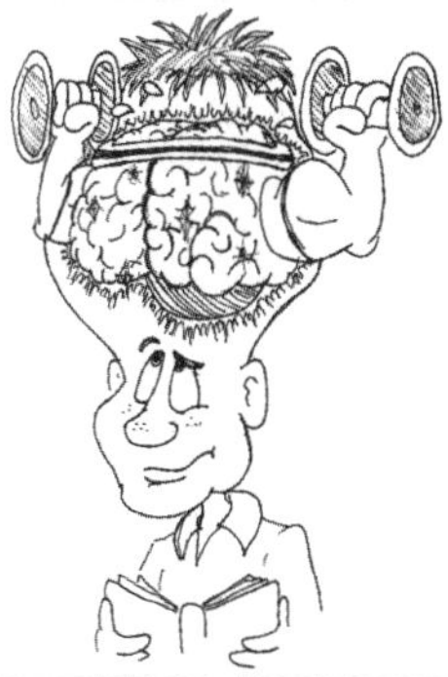

_____

_____

_____

_____

_____

_____

_____

_____

_____

_____

_____

_____

❝ _We're all pilgrims on the same journey, but some pilgrims have better road maps._ ❞

—Nelson DeMIlle

NEVER GIVE UP!!!

 **Lose Your Fear**

Many people stop before they reach their goals because they are afraid of what might happen along the way. What if I fail? What would happen if I actually reach my goals? If I go to college, will I have to leave behind my friends and family? What if I can't make it through high school?

FEAR has been described as:

F alse

E xpectations

A ppearing

R eal

If you see ten troubles coming down the road, you can be sure that nine will run into the ditch before they reach you.
—Calvin Coolidge

Most of the time, the things we are afraid of never actually happen. Your fear that nobody likes you just isn't true. If something does happen, it's usually not nearly as bad as you feared. If there is a challenge, you're prepared to handle it. You'll just practice your creativity and innovation skills to generate and implement solutions. What's one fear you have? Draw it inside the trash can above all the other fears.

CHAPTER FIVE

PARK THE JUDGE

Read the chapter to answer these preview questions.

{

Why do you need to Park the Judge?

What happens if you give in to peer pressure?

What is Direct Communication?

How do you know when someone is a Shifting Learner?

What is an example of a Negative Belief?

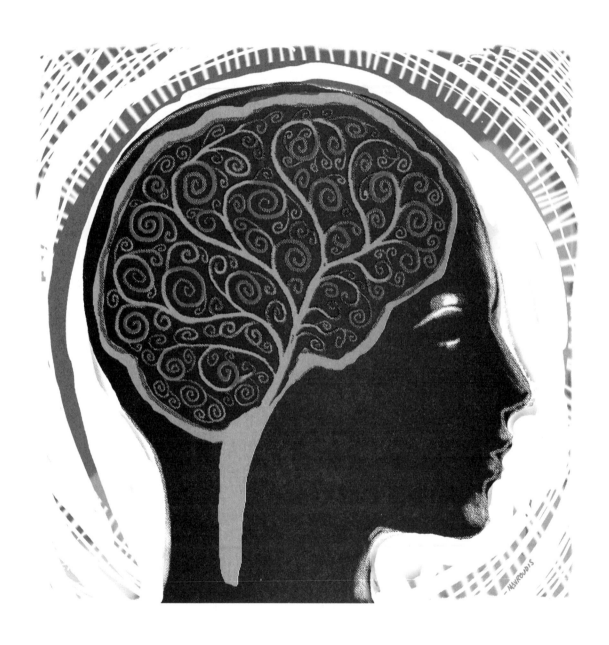

Park the Judge!

A recent college graduate started her own company and it was doing well. In a newspaper interview, she was asked how she was able to create such a successful company. "When I was in high school," she said, "I would come home after a challenging day filled with negative beliefs about myself: 'I'm not very smart,' or 'I can't pass biology,' or 'I'm not popular enough to win the election if I run for class president.' In response, very gently, my father would raise his hands in the air, and say firmly, 'Park the Judge.'"

"My father knew that if I kept judging myself, if I kept putting myself down, I wouldn't succeed. I needed to believe in my ability to reach my goals. The Judge kept getting in my way. Because of my father's reminders, I learned to recognize when I was judging myself, and then to park it. Now, whenever I have difficulties in running my company, and I start to judge myself, I remember what my father told me, and I tell myself: 'Park the Judge!' Once the Judge is parked, I can solve the problem more easily."

Each of us has a Judge inside. The Judge attacks us with the belief that we aren't good enough to reach our goals. The Judge attacks first and asks questions later. The Judge doesn't know if we are capable of reaching a goal (and doesn't care); its only purpose is to criticize us. Parking the Judge doesn't mean we'll be able to accomplish every goal we set. Nobody gets *everything* they hope to achieve. Parking the Judge means that we won't give up before we give ourselves an opportunity to reach our goals. When we allow ourselves to keep trying, and stay focused on reaching our goals, it is easier to move past the obstacles in our way.

> " Once the Judge is parked, I can solve the problem more easily. "

> It took me a long time not to judge myself through someone else's eyes.
> —Sally Field

 One strategy to park the Judge is to change the conversation. Focus on your action instead of listening to the Judge's criticism.

By ignoring (parking) the Judge, what action will you take to keep moving forward on your goals? Try this strategy out now on the next page.

In the left column are accusations often made by students' Judges. In each section of the left column, read the judgments. Then add an accusation made by your own Judge.

In the right column, list the action(s) you could take to move past the Judge and forward toward your goal.

JUDGE	I WILL... (TAKE ACTION)
I CAN'T go to college.	(example) I will choose three colleges to apply to and fill out the applications.
I CAN'T learn the 9 characteristics of living things.	
I CAN'T...	
I'M NOT smart enough to learn grammar rules.	
I'M NOT a good math student.	
I'M NOT ...	
I'M TOO tired to do any homework.	
I'M TOO new at this school to have friends.	
I'M TOO ...	

Negative Beliefs

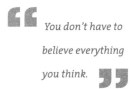

You don't have to believe everything you think.

The accusations of the Judge often keep us from moving forward to reach our goals. Negative beliefs we have about ourselves and other people can have the same impact. How many times have you believed something about another person, only to find out later that it wasn't true?

For example, maybe somebody tells you that another student has been making up lies about you. You might be angry and frustrated, and perhaps you even confront the other student. Or you might keep it to yourself, but feel upset or anxious when you hear this student's name because you believe that this student had been lying about you.

But what if it wasn't true? What if you created all your own upset or anxiety because of a negative belief? So many times it turns out that what we believed simply is not true. We create our worries based on our beliefs.

You don't have to believe every thought that passes through your brain. We have thousands of thoughts every day, and not all of them are true. Many thoughts are only opinions, inaccurate observations or just plain false ideas. Consider allowing yourself to observe your thoughts but not always believing them. Maybe it's all just crazy talk going on in your brain. You don't have to believe everything you think. Instead, when you have an upsetting or unproductive belief, try asking yourself these three questions:

1 Can I be certain that it's true?

2 What might happen if I act on this belief?

3 What else might I believe instead?

Suppose I believe the following:

"My science teacher doesn't care if I pass her class."

Can I be certain that it's true? What evidence do I have?
Most teachers really want students to pass the class, so it's
not likely to be true. But in order to answer this, you'd need
to look at the evidence: she hasn't offered to help me, and
she didn't call on me when I raised my hand. Can you be
certain that your teacher doesn't care if you pass based on
the evidence you list?

What might happen if I act on this belief? If you really
continued to believe that your teacher doesn't care if you
pass the class, you might decide that you don't care either
and stop trying. You might believe the same thing about
another teacher in another class.

What else might I believe instead? You might try believing:
"All my teachers want me to pass the class," or "What's most
important is whether I care about passing my class," or "If
my teacher doesn't call on me when my hand is raised, it
just means that my teacher was ready to call on another
student instead."

NEGATIVE BELIEF

*A belief is not an idea
held by the mind, it is
an idea that holds the
mind.*

—*Elly Roselle*

Try changing a Negative Belief

"Nobody can learn at this high school."

Small changes at the root of level of belief will produce amazing changes in behavior and performance.

—Harry Alder

1 Can I be certain that it's true? Do I have evidence?

....

2 What might happen if I act on this belief?

A ....

....

B ....

....

3 What might I believe instead?

A ....

....

B ....

....

Write down one of your negative beliefs:

....

....

1 Can I be certain that it's true? Do I have evidence?

....

2 What might happen if I act on this belief?

A ....

....

B ....

....

3 What else might I believe instead?

A ....

....

B ....

....

Write down another one of your negative beliefs:

....

....

1 Can I be certain that it's true? Do I have evidence?

....

2 What might happen if I act on this belief?

A ....

....

B ....

....

3 What might I believe instead?

A ....

....

B ....

....

Your present negative beliefs were formed by thought plus feelings.
—Maxwell Maltz

What happens if you give in to peer pressure?

- A 17 year-old girl joined her two friends in car surfing (riding on the hood, trunk or roof of a moving car). When she fell, she landed in critical condition at the hospital with a life-threatening head injury.

- Two teenagers persuaded each other that it was a good idea to light a large M80 firework that they had found. When it exploded, one of them lost most of his hand.

Why do students surrender to peer pressure? Why do they allow themselves to be talked into dangerous or illegal activities when they are with friends, even though they later recognize what a bad idea it was?

There are many reasons, but your brain plays an important role. In a recent study, psychologists discovered that peer pressure reduces teenagers' attention to risky behaviors. Their brains literally make poorer choices when their friends are with them. For example, teenagers who drive cars with friends in the car take more risks than when they drive alone.

You can't excuse poor choices by blaming your brain, however. There are many strategies that will improve your ability to make better choices. You can try any of these five strategies.

❶ Slow Down

One problem with poor choices is that they are choices made too quickly. Stop to think through your decision and to consider what might happen as a result. Try practicing patience; very few decisions actually need to be made immediately. Look at the possible bad outcomes if you make a sudden choice, and then just wait to make your decision later.

The Kaiser Foundation reports that nearly 50% of adolescents between the ages of 12 –18 feel pressured into having sex in relationships.

❷ Focus on Life Purpose & Values

It's much harder to give in to a friend's demand that you join her in surfing on the roof of a moving car if you focus on following your life purpose (sample Life Purpose: stay healthy, do well in high school and enjoy time with my family). Assuming you intend to stay alive (to be healthy) or spend time with family, falling from the top of a moving car is a choice that may not be aligned with your life purpose. If you value freedom, consider not surrendering your own freedom to follow a friend's bad idea.

❸ Your Strategy to Make Better Choices (add a new idea here that would work for you):

....

....

....

....

❹ Use the 4 Steps To Success

Return to the 4 Steps To Success decision-making process in Chapter Three to review (page 41).

JUMP!   JUST BECAUSE YOU DID IT DOESN'T MEAN I SHOULD

❺ Get a Mentor

When I dropped out of high school, I had a biology teacher who still believed in me. He believed in me more than I believed in myself at the time. We met several times to discuss the future, and he encouraged me not to give up on education. With his encouragement, I finally decided to enroll in a community college, and from there I eventually transferred to a university. At the university, I met a professor who offered me some suggestions on how to transfer to another university that had the program I needed to reach my goals. Within six months, I had transferred. At the new university, I had several wise mentors who helped me navigate the system. Their help made it much easier for me to succeed. I graduated, and as an educator myself, I have gone on to mentor many students to help them make better choices and reach goals.

Possible mentors can come from many areas in your life. Being mentored makes it easier for you to reach your goals. Consider getting yourself a mentor. How do you choose a mentor? You might look for someone who meets one or more of these criteria:

- Their values are similar to yours.

- You feel that you can really trust them.

- They have great listening skills and lots of life experience.

- They have a career that is related to your desired career.

- They graduated from a college/university that you'd like to attend.

In each of the following categories, identify one person who might serve as your mentor:

Family Member

....

Teacher or Counselor

....

Community Member/Elder

....

From these three options, choose one you will promise yourself to contact in the next week to request that they act as your mentor.

My Possible Mentor:

....

Direct Communication

Sometimes poor communication leads to poor choices. If you've ever overheard two people arguing, you might notice that they aren't really listening to each other. Their communication style is filled with accusations and judgment, poor listening, threats and making fun of people. When this communication style is used, it can lead to hurt feelings, fights and frustrating relationships.

Most people have found themselves stuck in a conversation like this at some point. Many people have conversations like this every week. There is another option for better communication, a method for more powerful and purposeful communication. Direct Communication asks speakers to communicate by identifying what happened, how they responded to it, and what they'd like instead.

• •

Tell the person what happened (Use an "I" statement)
I was asking a question in class and you talked over me.

Share your response (Use an "I" statement)
I was frustrated and confused.

Request what you'd like (Use an "I" statement)
I'd like to know that I can get an answer from the teacher to my questions without your interrupting, ok?

• •

Some Helpful Hints on Using Direct Communication

Tell the person what happened.
Do your best to just identify what actually happened, not your judgment about it (Park the Judge). "You were being a jerk" comes from the Judge, but "You grabbed my backpack and threw it down the hallway" is what actually happened. Stating what actually happened can help keep the situation from getting worse.

Share your response.
Use "I" language. Many people get stuck because they keep saying "You" instead of "I." Lead with an "I" statement. Instead of "You made me angry," try "I was angry." When you use "I" statements, you are communicating more powerfully, taking ownership of your response.

Request what you'd like.
Try to identify a reasonable solution to the situation. The other person might not agree to act on your suggestion. If not, you could ask that they come up with a reasonable solution. If you don't want to be angry any more, you might be able to solve the problem without the cooperation of the other person. This leaves you in the driver's seat, not relying on someone else to help you get what you'd like.

Try Out Direct Communication

Suppose another student had cut in front of you in the lunch line in the cafeteria.

Tell the person what happened:

....

....

....

Share your response:

....

....

....

Request what you'd like:

....

....

....

Positive Communication

Suppose a teacher had given you an "F" grade, insisting (wrongly) that you had turned in someone else's work.

Tell the person what happened:

....

....

Share your response:

....

....

Request what you'd like:

....

....

....

● ●

Suppose one of your brothers had taken your cell phone without your permission and left for the evening.

Tell the person what happened:

....

....

Share your response:

....

....

Request what you'd like:

....

....

What's the Point?

Write down 2 main points from this chapter (here or in your Road Log).

1 ....

....

....

2 ....

....

....

Create Your Road Log

Please record your learning and ideas in your Road Log.

If someone asked you to explain why you should "Park the Judge," write down how you would respond.

Three Learning Skills

As an ORGANIZING LEARNER, you learn well when you focus applying your organizational skills to an assignment or activity, for example:

- asking questions to understand directions
- using an outline
- sorting materials to order them before starting
- needing clear guidelines for a project
- prioritizing what needs to happen first

As an ACCEPTING LEARNER, you learn well when you follow an assignment or activity as it's presented by the teacher, for example:

- meeting deadlines consistently
- reaching agreement with the group or class
- carefully following assignment criteria
- not allowing mistakes to get you off track
- being open to other student opinions and ideas

As a SHIFTING LEARNER, you learn well when you suggest a different approach to assignments and activities, for example:

- offering a very different opinion on the assignment
- using a distinct approach in completing the assignment
- changing course quickly when circumstances change
- requesting a change in group roles for a project
- coming to different conclusions than other members of your group/class

Three Learning Skills: Organizing, Accepting and Shifting

Review the three learning skills on the opposite page. Students can learn new ideas and skills in many different ways. If you understand that you have many options and learning strategies, you can use more strategies to be a better learner.

A Number the three skills as follows: 1) the skill I prefer to use most often, 2) the skill I prefer to use sometimes, and 3) the skill I prefer to use least often.

1 ....

2 ....

3 ....

B Write down an example of how you have used one of the strategies from the skill you chose as #1. For instance, if you chose Shifting Learner, an example might be: I changed course quickly when the teacher added a new requirement to our life skills final project.

....

....

....

C Write down one way you could use one of the strategies from the skill you chose as #3. For instance, if you chose Accepting Learner, an example might be: I could meet deadlines consistently on English essay assignments.

....

....

....

Three students visited their high school counselor, Ms. Doomani. The first student told her: "I need to change my schedule since all my teachers are really bad." The second student said " I don't think I can make it through my algebra class." The third student had arrived late at her first period class two days in a row and had just come from after-school detention. When Ms. Doomani asked her why she had been late to school, she said: "I just can't get here by 8:20 a.m. every day."

Everything you want is out there ... but you have to take action to get it.
—Jules Renard

Which of these students has the most damaging belief, in your opinion? Which belief might lead the student to do something that would cause major problems? Explain.

....

....

....

....

If you were the high school counselor, what might you tell this student to help change his/her belief to a more effective one?

....

....

....

....

Uncool Facts

- 1/3 of high school students drop out of high school before getting a diploma.

- 1/3 of high school students graduate unprepared for college or a good job.

- 7000 middle & high school students drop out every day.

- Every year more than a million students do not graduate with their peers.

The statistics for middle and high school students are disturbing. However, these numbers do not represent your destiny, unless you choose to make it so. No matter which road you may have chosen in the past, you can choose a different road now. Use the strategies in *Choosing a Good Road* to create your intended life outcome.

In studies that look at whether high school students are ready to graduate high school and succeed in college, these are two of the important conclusions:

❶ Students who are already behind in academics when they begin high school are much more likely to drop out or fail to become college ready.

❷ Students who do not consistently attend school and fail classes during their first year of high school are unlikely to catch up—and often drop out.

No matter your past choices, you can make new choices now, and create different results. Try these strategies:

A **Find out your academic weaknesses and get help right away.** Ask your teachers or your counselor what you need to do to correct the problems. Do not delay in doing this.

B **Show up to school every day.** Come to every class (every day) unless you are sick.

C **Look for the early warning signs when you are doing poorly in a class.** Take action and ask for your teacher's help immediately if any of these are happening:

- You're failing quizzes and tests or not turning in assignments.

- You're not understanding what the teacher or other students are discussing, nor the concepts in the textbook.

- You're acting out by distracting yourself or the students in class.

"We must realize that we are all different in the way we perceive the world and use this understanding as a guide to our communication with others."—Anthony Robbins

Effective Communication

Misunderstandings at work are common. Problems with your customers, coworkers or employer can be created by simple communication problems. When a customer orders a steak sandwich and you bring a piece of chocolate cake, there was a misunderstanding. When your employer thinks you were supposed to work starting at 3 p.m., and you thought you were supposed to work at 5 p.m., there was a misunderstanding. When a coworker thinks you were supposed to clean the front windows, and you cleaned the back windows, there was a misunderstanding. Communicating can be made much easier by following a few simple guidelines.

Communicating with Employers

1 **Take Ownership:** Be accountable for your opinions and actions. Instead of saying "Nobody does that anymore," use an "I" statement: "I think we should offer a discount on the sandwiches on Wednesdays because two other restaurants are doing the same thing." Instead of saying, "Why is that floor so sticky?" try "I can clean it with a mop."

2 **Be Proactive:** When you see a problem, fix it. If you think you need permission to do so, then ask for it. Don't wait to be told to fix a problem. Your next conversation with your employer should communicate that you have taken action to solve a problem. Your words should persuade them that they can trust you to see and solve problems.

Communicating with Coworkers

1 **Be Empathic:** Empathy means you can really feel what someone else is feeling. If a coworker shares with you how frustrated he/she is about the new schedule, listen and take time to acknowledge the frustration. If you disagree instead, insisting that the schedule change is no problem, he/she won't feel like you understand his/her frustration.

2 **Reflect a Request:** If your coworker asks you to update the website with new pricing, reflect the request: "You'd like me to put the new prices from this update onto the home page of the website tonight?" If you do this, you can clarify what your coworker wants and be certain there is no misunderstanding. She might confirm your understanding, or she might say, "No, not tonight. We're not supposed to change the pricing until next week."

> If you can't have empathy and have effective relationships, then no matter how smart you are, you are not going to get very far.
> —Daniel Goleman

Communicating with Customers

1 **Adopt a Can-Do Attitude:** When a customer asks you for something, let the customer know you will find a way to get it done. If you think you're not supposed to do it, check with your employer, and ask for help in finding a way to meet the customer request, or ask your employer to explain what you can provide the customer. Part of your job is to help customers feel that you are there to help them out and that their requests are important.

2 **Be Positive:** Welcome all your customers and remember that they are the reason the company is in business. Employees with negative attitudes have a negative impact on the business. Instead of complaining about your job, or viewing customers as an interruption of your work, remember that your job depends on customers coming back in the future.

Positive Communication

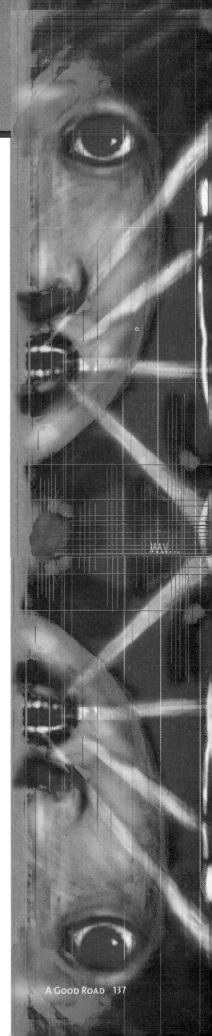

Listen to *Change Your Mind* by SISTER HAZEL. Look up the lyrics online. Explain the connection between Park the Judge and these lyrics from the song: "If you're tired of fighting battles with yourself, if you want to be somebody else, change your mind."

What did you learn?

I know you've learned a few important things!

_____

_____

_____

_____

_____

_____

_____

_____

_____

_____

_____

_____

❝ *There are only two mistakes one can make along the road to truth; not going all the way, and not starting.* ❞

—**Buddha**

NEVER GIVE UP!!!

 ## Change Your Negative Beliefs

Sometimes people give up on their goals because they doubt their abilities. They have a negative belief that gets in their way. For example, I might love to cook and want to open my own restaurant. Yet I might have the belief: "I'm not good with money. I could never run a restaurant." Until I change the negative belief, I probably won't take action on my goal.

The new (more effective) belief might be: "I can learn what I need to know about accounting," or "I could always hire someone to handle accounting for me." Don't let a negative belief get in your way. Try changing a belief right now. Think of a negative belief you carry about yourself, one that has gotten in your way before. For example:

Old Negative Belief: "I'm no good at spelling."

New Effective Belief: "Every time I practice spelling new words with flash cards, I get better at spelling."

Now you try it.

Your Old Negative Belief:

....

....

Your New Effective Belief:

....

....

Don't feed your mind with negative thoughts. If you do, you will come to believe them.
—Catherine Pulsifer

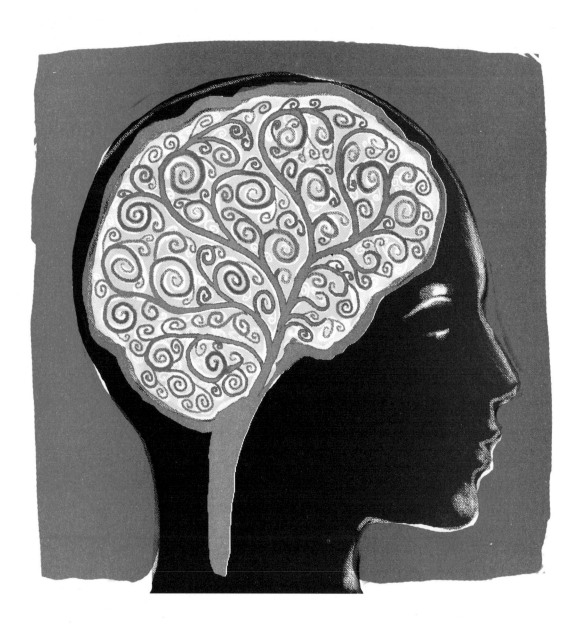

CHAPTER SIX

GOT TO GET IT TOGETHER

Read the chapter to answer these preview questions.

What is Lokahi?

What does it take to achieve unity?

Why should you set priorities?

What happens if you are missing balance in your life?

How do you know when someone is a Feeling Learner?

Setting & Acting on Priorities

Is it possible you could work hard ten hours a day and not accomplish anything important? Yes, if those ten hours were invested in doing things that were not your priorities. Working hard or working long hours is not enough to succeed. You need to work with intention. Working with intention means that you honor your life purpose, values and goals by prioritizing the actions that will help you fulfill your life purpose. You follow your values regularly and reach your goals often.

 To identify and set priorities, it's essential to keep focusing on your life purpose (Chapter 2), values and goals (Chapter 3). Write down your life purpose, 3 of your values and 3 of your goals.

Life Purpose

....

....

Values

1 ....

2 ....

3 ....

Goals

1 ....

2 ....

3 ....

SETTING PRIORITIES

Make a list of 10 things you plan to do tomorrow.

1 ....
2 ....
3 ....
4 ....
5 ....
6 ....
7 ....
8 ....
9 ....
10 ....

Looking back at your life purpose, 3 values and 3 goals, review the list to the left to decide what is really a priority.

Now re-write the list below in order of priorities, with #1 being the most important for the day.

MOST IMPORTANT PRIORITY

1 ....
2 ....
3 ....
4 ....
5 ....
6 ....
7 ....
8 ....
9 ....
10 ....

LEAST IMPORTANT PRIORITY

PURRING A PRIORITY? NO. MY TOP 3 ARE EATING, SLEEPING, AND CHASING CATS.

Organization & Efficiency

Once you get clear on your priorities, you need to act on them. To reach your goals, you need to make progress in getting things done. You need to be **ORGANIZED** so you can keep track of what needs to be done. You need to be **EFFICIENT** to get things done on time. Here are three rules for staying organized and being efficient:

Decide what you want; decide what you are willing to exchange for it. Establish your priorities and go to work.

—H. L. Hunt

1 Don't Delay.

Perhaps you've often heard, "I'll get around to it someday." How about today? If it's important to you, a priority, don't delay in taking action. When students put things off, they often fall further and further behind, until it's really hard to catch up. Handle important actions right away. If there are too many steps to get it done right away, take the first step, then put it on your Next Steps List.

2 What's Next? Next Steps!

Create a list of what you need to do, a Next Steps List, and keep moving through your list. If it's not important, not a priority, take it off your list and focus on what is important. As you complete each step, check it off the list. Keep adding to your Next Steps List when you have new goals or new steps to reach existing goals.

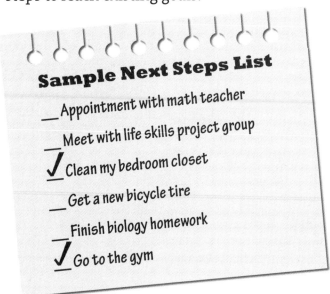

Sample Next Steps List

____ Appointment with math teacher

____ Meet with life skills project group

✓ Clean my bedroom closet

____ Get a new bicycle tire

____ Finish biology homework

✓ Go to the gym

3 Everything In Its Place...

The average employee spends about one week each year searching for misplaced items, and it costs companies about 90 billion dollars. Try this idea: everything has a place. Take the time to set up your study space, your computer desktop and your schoolwork so that you can find whatever you need. Decide the best place to file/hold anything you need, and then put everything in its place. Every day, take some time to put everything back in its place.

Draw your ideal study space, with everything neatly organized and all the tools you need to stay organized.

LOKAHI

Native Hawaiians believe Kupuna, honored elders or ancestors, are their source of traditional cultural beliefs, practices and values. One of the six important values handed down from Kupuna is **Lokahi**. Lokahi is a complex idea, and it includes achieving balance and ensuring unity. Working together, accepting responsibility, and doing what is right are all elements of Lokahi.

An example of Lokahi can be found in an important Hawaiian tradition, paddling outrigger canoes. Outrigger canoes have been used for many centuries by Hawaiians, and today outrigger canoe racing is the state sport. There are high school teams and outrigger canoe clubs found across the islands, and the canoes are popular with Hawaiians of all ages.

Most outrigger canoes hold 2-6 people, and the best way to paddle is by relying on Lokahi. Everyone must pay attention to what the others are doing, and everyone must paddle together or the canoe will slow down or go in the wrong

Six people in a canoe must work together to find a sense of balance, or the canoe, like a car with misfiring sparkplugs, will not move with grace in any direction, but falter in confusion. Lokahi means unity, and is fostered as each person learns to balance and moderate their strength, to a level that benefits everyone plus the canoe.

—Lokahi Canoe Club website

From the depth of need and despair, people can work together, can organize themselves to solve their own problems.

—César Chávez

Uncool Facts

- The average teenager now spends almost every waking hour (mostly when not in school) viewing a screen: using a smartphone, or on the computer or television.
- Teenagers with the highest levels of screen time can be at an increased risk of obesity.
- Teenagers with the most screen time were twice as likely to get C or lower grades in school.
- 50 percent of boys reported average total screen time above 42 hours per week.

direction. You can't win a canoe race by yourself; you must receive help from others. Unity and balance are both important. Everyone must stay united to keep the canoe moving correctly; there must be a balance between the strokes of the paddlers.

Lokahi is Unity

One day I broke my leg while playing soccer (ouch!). I had a cast for four weeks while it healed. I discovered that there was no way I could do what I needed to do without help. I couldn't carry anything heavy, so I needed to ask someone else to help me. I couldn't reach down to get anything I dropped (and I dropped a lot more things), so I asked for help. I couldn't use my crutches and also carry my lunch tray to a table, so I asked for help. When I asked for help, people helped me out. My biggest surprise was how many people offered to help me out, even when I didn't ask for help. You are surrounded by people who will help you. This is UNITY!

 Even if you don't have a cast or crutches, there are many things you cannot accomplish without asking for help.

If you are falling behind in biology class, you need help to get back on track. If your parents ask you to clean the entire yard, and you wait until you only have 20 minutes before guests arrive at your house for dinner, you need help. If you have a friend who tells you she started using drugs, you need help (she does too).

Helpers

In the center hexagon, write down an important goal, like improving your skills as shortstop on the softball team ("SHORTSTOP"). In the surrounding boxes, write in the names of people you might be able to ask for help.

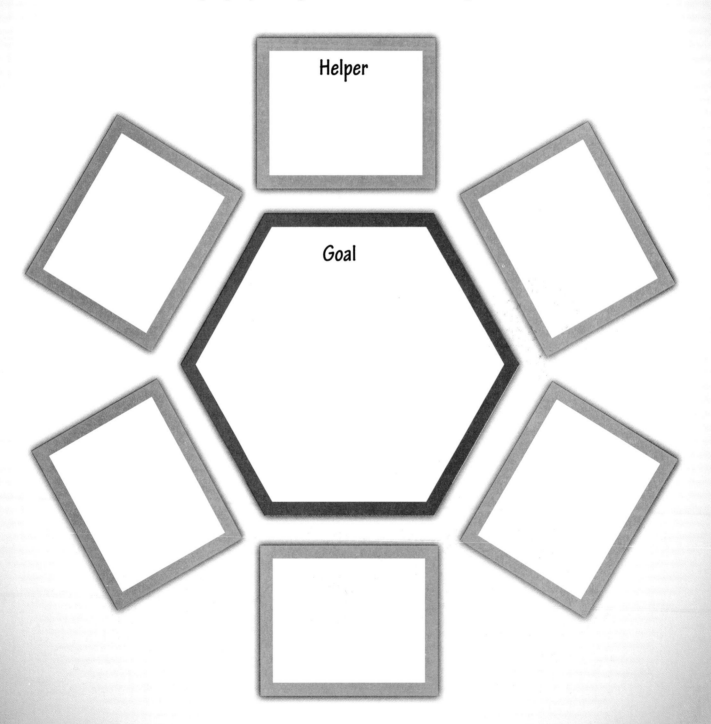

Organized?

Balanced?

What's the Point?

Write down 2 main points from this chapter (here or in your Road Log).

1 ....
....
....

2 ....
....
....

Create Your Road Log

Please record your learning and ideas in your Road Log.

If someone asked you to explain the concept of "Lokahi,"
write down how you would respond.

Lokahi is Balance

Just as with canoeing, life requires balance. If you have too much to do, you won't be able to give your best to anything. The average American watches more than thirty hours of television each week. With so many other important things to do in life, it's not likely that watching television for thirty hours is one of your highest priorities. With so much time spent on one low priority activity, there is less time to handle important things.

Some studies have shown teens spending over three hours a week instant messaging, over two hours weekly on YouTube, but only three hours a week using the internet for homework-related tasks.

■ Are you placing your highest priorities on your Next Steps list?

■ Do you have a balance between all your different priorities?

■ Are you certain you're moving forward on what's important?

To check on your life balance, fill in the boxes on the next page. In each box, write in one thing you do each week, and how many hours it takes (per week). See 3 sample boxes on the top of the page.

Are you investing the most time in activities that are the highest priorities? Do you have enough time each week to handle the highest priorities? Is there anything you might need to drop or change to stay in balance?

Beauty is only skin deep. I think what's really important is finding a balance of mind, body and spirit.

—Jennifer Lopez

Homework 9 hours	X-Box 3 hours	Volleyball 8 hours
	MY LIFE	

Three Learning Skills

As a THINKING LEARNER, you learn well when you examine facts and concepts of an assignment or activity, for example:

- asking questions to analyze ideas

- using facts to create an argument

- valuing your thoughts as the best way to understand something

- wanting to hear from experts in the field

- using critical thinking to build an argument

As a DOING LEARNER, you learn well when you are immediately active in an assignment or activity, for example:

- starting in right away to experience an activity

- valuing a clear understanding of how all the ideas are actually used

- improving the steps in the activity that is given to you

- focusing on what action needs to be taken next

- participating physically by moving around and touching things

As a FEELING LEARNER, you learn well when you pay attention to emotions when approaching assignments and activities, for example:

- relying on an emotional response as an important way to learn

- noticing connections between your life and the assignments

- discussing how others in the group feel as part of the learning process

- being highly aware of your changing emotions during an activity

- valuing storytelling and understanding teacher's experiences

Three Learning Skills: Thinking, Doing and Feeling

Review the three learning skills on the opposite page. Students can learn new ideas and skills in many different ways. If you understand that you have many options and learning strategies, you can use more strategies to be a better learner.

Good actions are a guard against the blows of adversity.
—*Abu Bakr*

A Number the three skills as follows: 1) the skill I prefer to use most often, 2) the skill I prefer to use sometimes, and 3) the skill I prefer to use least often.

1 ....

2 ....

3 ....

B Write down an example of how you have used one of the strategies from the skill you chose as #1. For instance, if you chose Feeling Learner, an example might be: I saw a connection between saving money for college and the lesson on compound interest in math class.

....

....

....

C Write down one way you could use one of the strategies from the skill you chose as #3. For instance, if you chose Doing Learner, an example might be: I could focus on what action needs to be taken next in my Spanish class.

....

....

....

ideas in action

Each of the students below has a challenge to address. Which of the effectiveness strategies do you think would best solve the student challenge? Draw a line from the student challenge in the left column to one or more of the best strategies in the right column.

Martin was feeling overwhelmed. Between school, his job, homework, soccer, baseball, watching tv, and hanging out with friends, he wasn't getting enough sleep and was tired and stressed.

Amy was trying to pass her biology class, but the textbook just didn't make any sense to her. Her parents were fighting at home, and her brother was skipping school and hanging out with his friends.

Rafael could never find anything. He lost his life skills textbook, his backpack was a disaster, and even when he did homework, he couldn't always find it.

Alicia was procrastinating on finishing her science project. There was a lot to do, and she also had tons of work to do to finish her study chart for Spanish. Instead of doing her work, she listened to music and read last year's yearbook.

Donnelle worked hard but never seemed to complete anything. He tried his best, but it was too hard to keep track of everything that needed to be done.

Tran spent 14 hours every week playing his favorite online game. He spent 12 hours weekly watching television, 3 hours doing homework and 6 hours at the mall watching people walk around and shop.

SETTING PRIORITIES

UNITY

BALANCE

DON'T DELAY

NEXT STEPS

EVERYTHING IN ITS PLACE

MAGA AND KEYA ON A GOOD ROAD

Reading Skills

First-year college students are sometimes surprised by the challenges of being a new student. Registering for the classes they need, getting used to a new setting, and understanding hundreds of pages of new ideas is not easy. In order to prepare for college, you'll need to be certain that your reading skills are very strong. To build sufficient myelin for strong reading skills, you'll need many hours of practice. Start now by trying out these reading strategies.

Be an Active Reader (interact with your textbook)

■ Look carefully at the Table of Contents in the front of the book or Index in the back to see what topics are included. Turn to this book's Table of Contents now and list 3 topics from Chapter Seven.

■ Scan the chapter headings for topics and try to answer any preview questions, or create your own preview questions. Return to this chapter's preview questions on page 141 and answer one now.

■ Ask questions of the textbook as you read: Why is this true? Who made this decision, and why? Write a question for this chapter:

> Don't ever dare to take your college as a matter of course—because, like democracy and freedom, many people you'll never know have broken their hearts to get it for you.
> —Alice Miller

- Agree or disagree with the author and some of the ideas in the textbook. Don't be a passive reader, but instead be an active reader and use your own judgment. Do you agree or disagree?

- Read the textbook more than once because it is very difficult to find all the important main points in the first reading. The more often you read, the more you will understand. Re-read these seven active reading strategies as soon as you reach the last one.

- Take notes while you read that include main points, evidence and examples, questions you have, and answers to preview questions. Turn to page 162 now to write down one thing you've just learned.

- Look up what you do not know, and write down terms to increase your vocabulary and understanding of concepts. Read the Malcolm X quote in the right margin and look up the phrase, *alma mater*.

"

My alma mater was books, a good library... I could spend the rest of my life reading, just satisfying my curiosity. —Malcolm X

"

Find the Thesis, Main Points and Details

The author's thesis, the overall main point, is most often found in the introduction to an essay, or at the beginning of a chapter. The thesis is the author's position, opinion or belief about the essay topic. The main points support the thesis in an argument essay. In an informational chapter, the main points are the key ideas to understand. Every main point is supported by details, such as evidence, examples and explanation. What is one main point from this page?

....

....

....

Summarize and Paraphrase

One key college skill is the ability to summarize the main ideas from any reading. If you want to do well when you are tested on a subject, or want to succeed in writing a paper about the topic, you'll need this skill. When you take notes while reading, organize the author's main points in outline form, listing these main points and several of the key details that support the points. Practice paraphrasing by explaining the author's point in your own words.

Many college students have problems with plagiarizing, which means copying the author's exact words without using quotation marks and citations (page numbers) or not giving the author credit for their original ideas. Don't plagiarize, or you can fail an assignment or class! When you paraphrase in your own words, you can avoid plagiarizing.

Understand and Analyze Arguments

Once you find the author's thesis (overall argument) and main points, analyze them. Is the author right or wrong? What evidence has been provided to support the main points? What strategies does the author use to create an argument? Is it a compelling argument? What would your position be? Why?

Paraphrase (in your own words) the paragraph above on understanding and analyzing arguments:

....

....

....

....

Don't Waste Your Time (or your employer's time)

Some employees use their time wisely. Some employees don't. American workers spend more than forty hours working each week, but many of those hours are not spent productively. Some workers report spending as little as 50% of their time doing job-related work, wasting time for up to twenty hours weekly.

Fill out the rest of the pie chart from the list below. Decide which non-job-related activities typical employees choose and what percentage of time they might waste.

For example, if you think 20% of time wasted at work is spent making personal phone calls, draw a slice that represents 20% of the pie and write "Personal Calls" and "20%" on the slice.

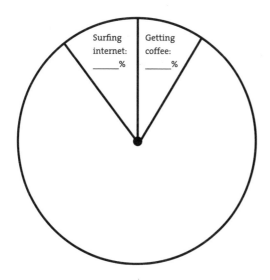

Surfing internet: ____ %

Getting coffee: ____ %

getting food

personal phone calls

sleeping

texting; emails

chatting with colleagues

> Analyzing what you haven't got as well as what you have is a necessary ingredient of a career.
> —Orison Swett Marden

> I do not want to waste any time. And if you are not working on important things, you are wasting time.
> —Dean Kamen

Workplace Facts

■ Time spent by each employee looking for lost items? 95 minutes per week or 76 hours per employee per year.

■ Cost? Almost 90 billion dollars.

■ 36% of employees waste 2 or more hours of time daily.

Identify 2 reasons to avoid wasting time at work:

A ....

....

B ....

....

If you were running your own business, identify 2 strategies you might use to persuade your employees to use their time wisely at work:

A ....

....

....

B ....

....

....

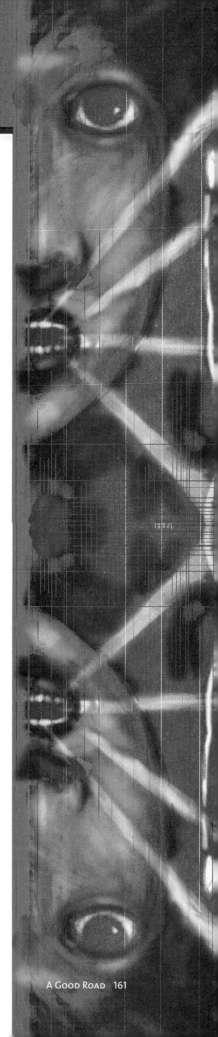

Watch and listen to *We Are the World Remix 25 for Haiti* (80 Guest Artists). Look up the lyrics online.

What other songs do you know that focus on unity?

Artist: ....
Song: ....

Artist: ....
Song: ....

If your school was to adopt a theme song with a message promoting unity, what song would you chose?

....

Why would you choose this song to promote unity?

....

....

....

....

What did you learn?

I know you've learned a few important things!

If you don't know where you are going, any road will get you there.

— Lewis Carroll

NEVER GIVE UP!!!

It's a long old road, but I know I'm gonna find the end." **—Blues singer Bessie Smith**

Promise Yourself

Here's another idea to get what you want: **Promise yourself that you'll make it happen no matter what**! What would happen if you ran out of excuses about why you couldn't reach a goal? Making a promise is a way of bypassing excuses, choosing a better road. Make keeping a promise more important than giving in to an excuse.

· *List one of your most important future goals:*

....

What excuses might you have made in the past for not reaching this goal?

....

....

....

*Write down a promise you are willing to make to yourself about never giving up on this goal (in **BIG, BOLD** writing).*

....

....

....

People with integrity do what they say they are going to do. Others have excuses.
—Laura Schlessinger

Each morning I gaze at the eastern horizon, and if the sun keeps its promise, I keep mine.
—Robert Brault

Promise a lot and give even more.
—Anthony J. D'Angelo

CHAPTER SEVEN

CREATIVE AND CRITICAL THINKING

Read the chapter to answer these preview questions.

What are the creativity competencies?

What happens if you are missing creativity in your life?

What does it take to demonstrate critical thinking?

Why should you be able to manage diversity in your life?

How do you know when someone is a Writing Learner?

Creativity & Learning

Perhaps we all started out as small children being highly creative, but at some point, many people appear to set aside their creativity. Creativity can mean the ability to create an original work of art, but it also means approaching life with creativity. When you ignore your creativity, you ignore your ability to generate original and effective solutions to the many challenges life will throw your way.

 To get past the obstacles that might prevent you from graduating high school and getting into college, you need to rely on creativity.

Here are three creativity competencies you can improve.

1 Ability to generate multiple options or solutions

People who get stuck think they have run out of possible answers. The more options you generate, the more options you have to choose from. The more options to choose from, the more likely you are to find an option that works as an effective solution. People who tap into their creativity can generate dozens, hundreds or thousands of possible options or solutions.

2 Ability to see/hold many perspectives

As Albert Einstein once said, we need to "regard old problems from a new angle" if we want to find solutions. If you haven't solved a challenge yet, you might need to try something new. Too often we get stuck in old habits and patterns. In order to see a new solution, we need to get unstuck, going well beyond our limited perspective to see the challenge from another perspective.

3 Willingness to risk being "wrong"

It's important to take healthy risks, and especially to risk being wrong. Life has a lot to teach us when we step outside of our comfort zone and try something new. Students who take a risk and get things wrong can get to right answers more quickly. They can learn valuable lessons from the mistakes they made. If you're not making mistakes, not taking healthy risks, you're not maximizing your learning.

• •

Practice your ability to generate multiple options or solutions

Generate some options or possible solutions to the problem described below:

Problem: Sharon has been unable to get to her first period class on time. If she doesn't solve the problem, she will end up in detention, or worse, not pass her class. Her younger brother has to be at elementary school at 8:20 a.m. It takes 20 minutes to get from her brother's school to Sharon's high school, and Sharon's first period starts at 8:30. Her mom isn't willing to drop off Sharon's brother earlier since he's much younger than Sharon and the teachers don't supervise the children until school starts. She can't drop off Sharon at 7:55 or 8:00 because the high school gates don't open until 8:05. Generate options to solve this problem.

Option/Solution 1

....

....

....

To raise new questions, new possibilities, to regard old a from a new angle, requires creative imagination and marks real advances in science.
—*Albert Einstein*

Inside you there's an artist you don't know about...Say yes quickly, if you know, if you've known it from the beginning of the universe.
—*Rumi*

They are ill discoverers that think there is no land, when they can see nothing but sea.
— *Francis Bacon*

Option/Solution 2

....

....

Option/Solution 3

....

....

....

Option/Solution 4

....

....

....

Option/Solution 5

....

....

....

PROBLEM SOLVING

Practice your ability to see/hold multiple perspectives

Sometimes it is hard to solve a challenge because everyone sees the world in such a different way. For example, many families have a challenge with rules about watching television or other technology screen time. Parents want less screen time and kids often want more. Recall some of the information from Chapter 6 about the outcomes of excessive screen time. Teenagers with the highest levels of screen time can be at an increased risk of obesity, and teenagers who spend the most time on a screen are twice as likely to get C or lower grades in school. Now put yourself into another's shoes. Thoughtfully write down what you sincerely believe this family's positions to be on the issue of screen time. Assume that everyone has a valid perspective and that everyone only wants the best for the family.

Martin (15 years old) believes...

....

....

....

Deborah (10 years old) believes...

....

....

....

Martin and Deborah's mom believes...

....

....

....

Imagination is more important than knowledge.
—*Albert Einstein*

The uncreative mind can spot wrong answers, but it takes a very creative mind to spot wrong questions.
—*Anthony Jay*

Martin and Deborah's dad believes...

....

....

....

Martin's teacher believes...

....

....

....

Martin and Deborah's grandmother believes...

....

....

....

Can you suggest a fair solution that takes all these perspectives into account?

....

....

....

Practice your willingness to risk being "wrong"

Make a Mistake

Many students play it safe. They don't want to be seen by others as being "wrong" or, even worse, "dumb." So they play it safe, keeping quiet if they're not certain of an answer to a teacher's question, or not contributing their ideas when it seems like it might be a risk.

Creativity is allowing yourself to make mistakes. Art is knowing which ones to keep.
—Scott Adams

And the trouble is, if you don't risk anything, you risk even more.
—Erica Jong

Research says that you learn better when you are willing to attempt "wrong" answers. The wrong answers turn out to be the best pathway to learning how to do something correctly. Many great inventors have gotten it wrong hundreds of time before they get it right. But just because the research says it's a good idea to let yourself try out wrong answers doesn't mean you will, especially if you have a negative belief that stops you. Write a negative belief below about the consequences of getting it wrong.

Negative Belief: If I get it wrong, then…

....

....

....

If you were to create a new belief that would give you permission to risk getting it wrong, what would it be?

New Belief: If I get it wrong, then…

....

....

....

Now it's time to risk being wrong about something. Try to answer the question below, even if you don't know the answer. Take a risk that you might get it wrong.

Challenging Question: How many high school students drop out of high school every day in the United States?

....

More Challenging Question: Why do so many students drop out every day?

....

....

....

Take calculated risks. That is quite different from being rash.

—*General George S. Patton*

(Okay: after you risk giving your own answers, you can find some useful information in the textbook on pages viii and 132, or search the internet to see what else you can discover.)

● ●

Healthy Risks...or Big Risks?

What is a healthy risk? Some risks are worth taking and some are not. You need to decide which are appropriate Healthy Risks and which are just plain dangerous Big Risks. Here's a method to calculate risk:

Will there be a Positive or Negative Outcome?

A Positive Outcome means that you safely reach a desired goal. For example, a positive outcome might mean that you risk asking your math teacher for extra help in learning how to multiply fractions, and then you learn how to multiply fractions by yourself. This is probably a healthy risk.

A Negative Outcome means that you do not reach a desired goal, and that you also experience an undesired outcome as a consequence of the big risk you took. For example, a negative outcome might mean that you take a big risk by climbing over the stadium fence to get to the homecoming football game. When you get caught sneaking in, the security guard files a report with the school vice-principal, calls your parents to pick you up, and you don't get to see the game.

To practice calculating whether something is a Healthy Risk or Big Risk, analyze and categorize the risks on the next page:

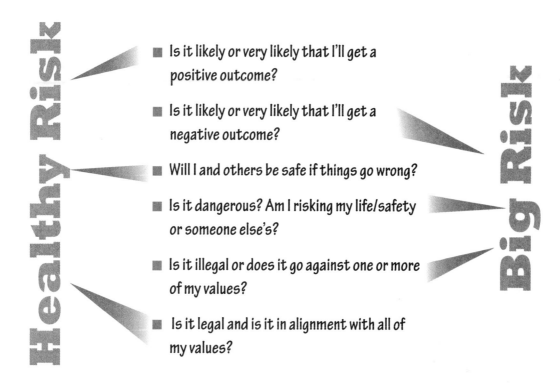

Healthy Risk

- Is it likely or very likely that I'll get a positive outcome?
- Is it likely or very likely that I'll get a negative outcome?
- Will I and others be safe if things go wrong?
- Is it dangerous? Am I risking my life/safety or someone else's?
- Is it illegal or does it go against one or more of my values?
- Is it legal and is it in alignment with all of my values?

Big Risk

Categorize the following risks as a Healthy Risk or a Big Risk:

Healthy Risk		Big Risk
☐	take an elective	☐
☐	try a really hard extra credit question on the quiz	☐
☐	make friends with a new student	☐
☐	start in on your woodshop project without required safety glasses	☐
☐	text in class	☐
☐	buy drugs on school grounds after school	☐
☐	try out for the school musical	☐
☐	ask your geometry teacher for help	☐
☐	skip a class to leave school and get a sandwich	☐
☐	show up to class without homework	☐
☐	run for school president in your first year	☐
☐	answer a question when you're not 100% certain of the answer	☐
☐	violate the school dress code	☐
☐	arrive late to class	☐
☐	try a new dance move out at the homecoming dance	☐
☐	yell at the principal when she asks you why you're late	☐
☐	try to beat your own record for number of pushups in 5 minutes	☐
☐	bully a student who annoys you	☐
☐	sneak into the swimming pool when it's closed	☐

What is the next Healthy Risk you might take to reach one of your goals?

....

....

....

• •

Critical Thinking Skills

What is critical thinking? It is thinking that demonstrates several specific abilities:

- to understand the various sides of an issue
- to see clearly how each side's arguments are made
- to be able to respond with well-constructed arguments of your own

Why is critical thinking important? Imagine that you go to your favorite pizza joint for a slice. After you order, the cashier tells you, "That will be $25.00." *What?*, you think. *$25.00 for one slice of pizza? It was $2.95 just last week.* "It's really good pizza," the cashier says. "Besides, the cost of cheese went way up." Not using critical thinking skills, you might just hand over $25.00. Using strong critical thinking skills, you might start asking a lot of questions instead: "Isn't it only 20 cents worth of cheese anyway? Even if cheese doubled in price, wouldn't that only be an extra 20 cents?" "How could you expect to stay in business if you charge $25.00 for a slice of pizza?" "Are you sure you didn't charge me for the triple king family size pizza combination with everything on it and 4 sodas and bread sticks? I see on the menu that it costs $25.00." "Oh yeah," the cashier says, "I must have pushed the wrong key on the register."

Practice Critical Thinking

Situation: Jasmine and Latoya got into an argument after school. Jasmine said that Latoya got in her face about nothing, and that Latoya accused her of copying Latoya's homework assignment for English. Latoya said that Jasmine was exaggerating because she didn't get closer than three feet from Jasmine. Besides, the teacher told her that Jasmine's homework had the exact same answers to the practice questions as hers! Jasmine said that it didn't matter if they had the same answers, and besides Latoya got way too close to her and was disrespectful.

Jasmine's Major Arguments:	Latoya's Major Arguments:

Evidence Jasmine Presents:	Evidence Latoya Presents:

Write your own well-constructed argument here. Analyze the problem(s) and suggest a fair solution.

....

....

....

....

....

....

●●●●●●●●●●●●●●●●●●●●●●●●●●●●●●●●●●●

Diversity Awareness & Management

It's a diverse world, and it is getting more diverse each day. This means we interact with people from many different backgrounds. We will continue to be surrounded by a diverse population, whether they are employers, customers, students, teachers, neighbors, or family members.

Managing this increasing diversity well means having some effective diversity strategies. These strategies can be a combination of critical and creative thinking approaches which include these abilities:

1. to understand the various sides of an issue
2. to see/hold multiple perspectives
3. to see clearly how each side's arguments are made
4. to be able to respond with well-constructed arguments of your own

Diversity Case Study

David, Corinne and Fernando agreed one Saturday morning to meet for dinner that night. "What time?" texted David. "Around 5" replied Corinne. Fernando replied: " ☺ "

At 4:50, David showed up at El Portal restaurant. He waited for his friends until 5:09, then he ordered his dinner. A minute later Corinne arrived. "Hey, I'm hungry" she said, "Let's order."

David said, "I already did." Corinne replied, "You didn't wait. You must have been really hungry." David said, "That's right," but he was upset with Corinne.

After dinner, at 5:45, David said: "I guess Fernando blew us off." Corinne replied, "I don't think so; he's just running on Fernando time." "Really," said David, "What time are you running on?" Corinne protested: "I said I'd be here around 5, and I was!" David said, "I was here to meet you before 5. You showed up late. Fernando didn't come at all. In my family, 5 means 5, or even earlier to be sure we're exactly on time."

Corinne replied, "In my family, when we say around 5, it means a little after 5, not exactly at 5. If my family invites you to dinner and you show up early, we might not even have the table set. My mom gets mad when people show up early. She says they don't have any manners." David looked like he had no idea what Corinne was talking about. Just then Fernando walked up, smiling broadly.

"Dude, it's 5:48, said David. Where were you? We already ate."

Fernando replied: "You didn't wait for me? It's not even 6 yet. I texted you guys this morning." "Yeah," said David, "but you never showed." "Well here I am," said Fernando. "I'm even early since in my family, showing up at 5 normally means showing up between 6 and 7."

David shook his head. Corinne shrugged her shoulders. Fernando didn't understand why his friends didn't wait for him. The three friends all left, disappointed and not fully understanding each other.

Has a misunderstanding like this ever happened to you? Explain.

....

....

....

....

....

Which diversity strategy would be most useful in this situation? Why?

....

....

....

....

....

....

Diversity

What's the Point?

Write down 2 main points from this chapter (here or in your Road Log).

1 ....

....

....

2 ....

....

....

Create Your Road Log

Please record your learning and ideas in your Road Log.

If someone asked you to explain the importance of creativity, write down how you would respond.

Three Learning Skills

As a SPEAKING LEARNER**, you learn well when you can speak to others to contribute ideas when completing an assignment or activity, for example:**

- making a presentation to the class

- debating ideas with other students

- having a paired discussion

- testing through an oral examination

- creating an audiovisual learning clip to upload

As a WRITING LEARNER**, you learn well when you can write down ideas when completing an assignment or activity, for example:**

- taking notes during short lectures

- writing a letter to an historical figure

- developing a composition

- writing a short in-class essay

- journaling to record your reflections on learning

As a READING LEARNER**, you learn well when you can read your own and others' ideas when completing an assignment or activity, for example:**

- reading a textbook chapter to prepare for a quiz

- relying on class handouts to understand concepts

- valuing a lecture that is accompanied by a PowerPoint

- editing another student's writing

- reading and reviewing your own notes to prepare for a test

Three Learning Skills: Speaking, Writing and Reading

Review the three learning skills on the opposite page. Students can learn new ideas and skills in many different ways. If you understand that you have many options and learning strategies, you can use more strategies to be a better learner.

A Number the three skills as follows: 1) the skill I prefer to use most often, 2) the skill I prefer to use sometimes, and 3) the skill I prefer to use least often.

1 ....

2 ....

3 ....

B Write down an example of how you have used one of the strategies from the skill you chose as #1. For instance, if you chose Writing Learner, an example might be: I stopped to record my reflections on cell walls in biology.

....

....

....

C Write down one way you could use one of the strategies from the skill you chose as #3. For instance, if you chose Speaking Learner, an example might be: I could debate the risks of sexual activity with other students in health class.

....

....

....

ideas in action

Each of these students has a challenge to solve. Should they use creative thinking or critical thinking to do so? Explain why.

Challenge	Creative or Critical?	Explain Why
Ana is failing all of her classes. She hasn't done any studying and doesn't always come to school.		
Talulah has missed 4 weeks of school because her aunt asked her to stay home and watch her aunt's new baby.		
Sergio's father is an alcoholic and sometimes when he drinks, he hits Sergio's mother and brothers.		
Scott is homeless because his parents both lost their jobs and then they lost their home.		
Rossi's Spanish teacher is never prepared for class. She forgets to bring assignments and doesn't explain lessons clearly.		
Viet has already been sent to detention 10 times for talking back to teachers and coming late to classes.		

> I think a college education is important no matter what you do in life.
> —Phil Mickelson

Depth and Rigor

Some high school students learn only a little bit about a lot of different topics. Research suggests that you will be better prepared for college if you learn with depth and rigor, developing greater mastery of your subject areas.

Depth of understanding means you know more about your subject so you can include more details and examples in your arguments. You will be more confident and clear about your subject. **Rigor** ensures that you know your subject area well enough to be accurate in your understanding.

You will be an expert if you have developed depth and rigor in your approach to learning. Here are some strategies for depth (knowing more) and rigor (accurate understanding).

1. Stick with it longer.

2. Review more often.

3. Practice and build myelin.

4. Ask "Why?"

① Stick with it longer.

Some students quit trying when they face a challenge. Then they miss out on learning that gives them a depth of understanding of their topic. Schedule enough time to do your work fully and completely without rushing. Keep trying even if you are bored, frustrated or lack confidence. The only way to build confidence is through sticking with it until you understand it.

② Review more often.

If you wait a few weeks before reviewing your notes and readings, you'll forget about 80% of the ideas. Reviewing more often increases how much you remember. Review within 24-48 hours after taking notes or reading, then schedule short review sessions 2-3 times weekly.

③ Practice and build myelin.

You've learned that Effective Practice builds myelin. Look for opportunities to practice until you gain greater confidence in what you're doing. If only a few problems are assigned, try doing the entire problem set. Double your time spent practicing skills. Increase your accuracy in solving problems.

④ Ask "Why?"

Frequently asking the question "Why?" means you are an active learner, not a passive learner. Passive learners are content to learn a little bit about a topic, but active learners insist on a deeper understanding. Asking questions like "Why?" will inspire you to look for answers, thus increasing your mastery of the topic.

> In the depth of winter I finally learned that there was in me an invincible summer.
> —Albert Camus

Ranking & Coaching

The following are the major reasons employees lose their jobs. Rank them in order of the most serious problem (1) to the least serious problem (7), giving each a different number.

_____ Lying at work or being dishonest on a resume

_____ Missing work

_____ Refusing to do what the boss requests

_____ Talking too much and conducting personal business at work

_____ Not getting along with colleagues

_____ Not completing assigned tasks on time

_____ Drug and alcohol abuse

Using the one you decided was the most serious problem (#1), coach the employee by offering three suggestions for how he or she might solve the problem.

1 ....

....

2 ....

....

3 ....

....

Choose four or five of your favorite songs from your music library. Find a place you can listen and focus. While you are listening, pick up a pencil, pen, paintbrush or anything else you want to use to be creative. Write, draw, paint, or create anything you want. Stay focused and aware of how it feels to be creative. Repeat as needed.

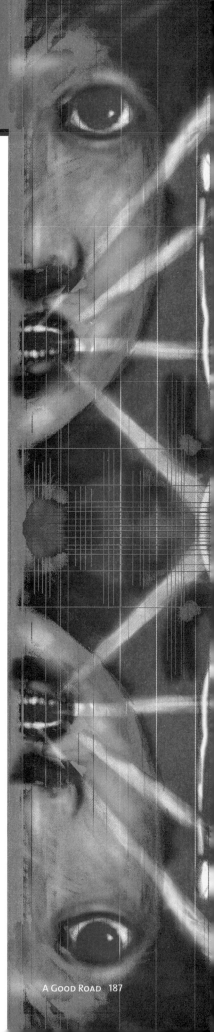

What did you learn?

I know you've learned a few important things!

The road to success, and by that I mean... the possibility of giving the best one has to the cause that one loves most, is not easy.

—Louis Finkelstein

NEVER GIVE UP!!!

 What appears to be the end of the road may simply be a bend in the road. —Robert H. Schuller

Find Another Way

You've tried again and again. Your approach doesn't seem to solve your challenge. It's not working. Maybe it's an opportunity to take some time to reflect on what happened, even to accept that it won't work. You may have to simply accept that no matter how hard you try, the approach is not working. It may be time to give up. Is there a goal you have given up on before, an impossible goal? Write it here:

Impossible goal:

....

What I tried:

....

....

Though your approach may not be working, don't ever give up on an important life goal. Give up on the ineffective approach. There are many roads to the same destination. It's time to find another way. Try three new strategies.

❶ Clarify the Goal

Figure out what you really need. Sometimes we don't reach a goal because it is not what we really need. Instead of "I can't get my little brother to be quiet," I can find my deeper need (my true goal), to experience more quiet, and find out many other ways to get what I need. For example, I could leave the house and study at a friend's house.

We can't solve problems by using the same kind of thinking we used when we created them.
—**Albert Einstein**

It is not enough for a man to know how to ride; he must know how to fall.
—**Mexican Proverb**

② **Look at What Others Have Done**

If anyone else in the entire history of the world has reached
this goal, that means there is a way to do so. Examine what
others have done to reach the goal and then try it yourself.
Try a new approach by using the Four Steps to Success
process (page 40) to generate some new options.

③ **Recommit to the Goal**

Once you have decided you won't give up, try a new
strategy every week until you find one that works. Just
don't give up, even if it takes many years. Some of our most
essential goals cannot be achieved in a week, a month or
even a year. Sometimes an essential goal takes many years
to achieve. Never give up.

New Commitment:

....

....

....

....

Drawing of you reaching your goal:

CHAPTER EIGHT

BE A LEADER

Read the chapter to answer these preview questions.

What does creativity have to do with leadership?

Why should you use effective listening skills?

What happens when a student doesn't use the 5 Rules of Effective Leadership?

How do you know when someone is a Watching Learner?

What does it take to demonstrate leadership?

Leadership

Are you a leader? Can others count on you to help them reach a goal? Do you have the leadership skills that are required to succeed in life?

Leadership and learning are indispensable to each other.

—John F. Kennedy

It is better to lead from behind and to put others in front.

—Nelson Mandela

A leader takes people where they want to go … a great leader takes people where they don't necessarily want to go, but ought to be.

—Rosalynn Carter

Leadership is your ability to organize and inspire others (and yourself) to move forward to reach important goals.

Write down your definition of leadership:

....

....

....

Developing your mastery of concepts from biology, geometry and English is very important. Yet there is more to learn in high school than academic concepts. It's also very important to develop mastery in leadership skills. You can learn how to lead others to accomplish crucial projects, a skill you'll need to use frequently in your career. You'll need strong leadership skills to stay true to your values.

You'll also need to demonstrate leadership if you play sports, as well as in your community, in the classroom and in your home. How will you learn to do all this?

Fortunately, you're already a step ahead in learning leadership skills. Many of the strategies you've been learning in this textbook are leadership skills. Review the following ten skills from the book and write down how they could be used as leadership skills.

Good Road Strategies	*Used as Leadership Skills*
Knowing your Life Purpose	Lead a service project that is a match for my life purpose
Flexibility and Adaptability	
Setting Goals	
Following Your Values	
Having a Growth Mindset	
Responding to Peer Pressure	
Setting Priorities	
Achieving Unity	
Using Creativity	
Using Critical Thinking	

Leadership

You are already an expert in leadership because you've already been a leader at some point in your life.

When have you helped others reach a goal? When have you been courageous enough to keep going when facing a big challenge? When have you believed in other people's ability to get the job done, even when they quit believing? When have you encouraged others to do their best? When has your behavior served as a model for other people? When you've been a leader, that's when!

When have you already demonstrated leadership in your life? Give some examples below:

• •

In the classroom

• •

At the school

• •

In your family

• •

In your community

• •

Nobody can dim the light which shines from within.
—Maya Angelou

Moving fast is not the same as going somewhere.
—Robert Anthony

Leadership is getting players to believe in you. If you tell a teammate you're ready to play as tough as you're able to, you'd better go out there and do it.
—Larry Bird

LEADERSHIP

Demonstrating Leadership

You've already learned some leadership skills. You've already demonstrated your leadership ability. There are big problems to be solved in this world, at your school and in your community. Your leadership skills are needed. What will you do now?

Check each area where you are willing to take leadership.

- ☐ In the classroom
- ☐ At school
- ☐ In sports
- ☐ At your job
- ☐ In your family
- ☐ In your community

In one leadership area you chose, identify a Leadership Role you could take (for example, conflict mediator; volunteer; team captain):

• •

Leadership Role

• •

Set a Leadership Goal for this role (for example, family working together; everyone on team contributing). Draw a representation below.

More Leadership Skills: Effective Listening

If you want to be really effective as a leader, one skill may rise above all others: listening. Here are some effective listening strategies:

❶ Don't Talk. Just Listen. Let someone vent, share, or request something. Don't interrupt them, or give them advice or disagree with them. When they stop, ask them to share more ("What else?" or "Boy, that sounds really hard!")

❷ Pay Attention to Body Language. Show them you care about what they have to say. People can read your body language: your arms crossed or unfolded, your body turned toward them or away from them, rolling your eyes or raising your eyebrows, raising your hands, and giving eye contact. Research on communication notes that less than 10% of your communication comes from the actual words you use. Be aware of what your body language is communicating to the person who is speaking to you. Be aware of what the speaker's body language is communicating to you, along with their words.

❸ Repeat Back What You Hear. Speak back to them what you think they've just said and allow them to correct your understanding ("So, you're feeling really angry right now?" "No, I'm actually really scared.") Do this authentically and not like a parrot or robot. Get accurate information. People know when you are listening to, caring about and understanding what they actually said.

Try It Now. Go try these skills with the very next friend who talks to you.

Report Back. Return to this page and write down what you experienced and learned from using Effective Listening. What did you try? How did they respond? What did you learn?

My Experience & Learning

....

....

....

....

....

....

Listen and be led.

—*L. M. Heroux*

A good listener is not only popular everywhere, but after a while he gets to know something.

—*Wilson Mizner*

Deep listening is miraculous for both listener and speaker. When someone receives us ... our spirits expand.

—*Sue Patton Thoele*

Service Learning

One powerful way to demonstrate your leadership is through service learning. Service learning is the opportunity to contribute to others while learning important lessons. If you are studying blood types in biology, you might volunteer at a medical clinic. If you are studying nutrition, you could help prepare meals at a food kitchen to feed homeless people. If you play on the lacrosse team, you might volunteer to coach younger teams or help build a new field in your town. Here's what a few other students have done:

- Students at Telstar Middle & High School in Maine set a goal to improve the health of the local community by using the school gardens and greenhouse to grow food and by working with local farmers. (http://gotfarms.wordpress.com/)

- A student named Andy at W.T. Woodson High School in Virginia volunteered to referee during the Special Olympics championship games. (http://www.fcps.edu/woodsonhs/service/archives.html)

- Students at New Vista High School in Colorado leave the school early each Wednesday to volunteer in the Community Experience Program. These opportunities include internships working with architects, artists, restaurants, skate shops, hotels, or other schools. (http://www.publicschoolreview.com/school_ov/school_id/13850)

List two things you could do to be of service at your school:

❶ ....

❷ ....

List two things you could do to be of service in your community:

❶ ....

❷ ....

Now that you've identified two things you could do to be of service in your community or at your school, it's time to create an Action Plan. You don't have to follow through on this plan (it's your choice of course). Perhaps you will join others, discuss a plan with your teacher and do something together as an entire class. No matter what you choose, it's helpful to have an action plan so you are clear on the steps and goals of the project.

Action Plan

1 Who do you need to contact to set this up?

....

2 What excites you about giving to others in this project?

....

....

3 Who else could join you on this project?

....

....

4 What would you like to accomplish (goals)?

....

....

5 Who will you turn to if you get stuck in moving forward (mentor)?

....

6 What's your first step?

....

No act of kindness, no matter how small, is ever wasted.

—Aesop

It is only in the giving of oneself to others that we truly live.

—Ethel Percy Andrus

What we learn to do, we learn by doing.

—Aristotle

From what we get, we can make a living; what we give, however, makes a life.

—Arthur Ashe

We are the leaders we have been waiting for.

—Sweet Honey and The Rock

To lead the people, walk behind them.

—Lao Tzu

What's the Point?

Write down 2 main points from this chapter (here or in your Road Log).

1 ....

....

....

2 ....

....

....

Create Your Road Log

Please record your learning and ideas in your Road Log.

If someone asked you to explain the qualities of effective leadership, write down how you would respond.

Three Learning Skills

As a LEADING LEARNER, you learn well when you can take charge of a learning experience, for example:

- taking a leadership role in a group project

- leading a class discussion

- assigning roles to other students in a lab setting

- asking a series of questions of the teacher

- directing a class demonstration or school play

As a TRYING LEARNER, you learn well when you can try something yourself when completing an assignment or activity, for example:

- going up to the board to solve a problem

- reading directions to understand an activity without a teacher's direction

- trying it yourself before accepting an offer of help

- taking a hands-on approach to your learning

- experimenting by predicting possible outcomes

As a WATCHING LEARNER, you learn well when you can watch others trying something out before you complete an assignment or activity, for example:

- watching the teacher solve a sample problem before trying it

- asking for a demonstration of a new skill from a coach

- valuing the learning that comes from viewing a video

- taking notes and trying something later on your own

- writing a reflection of what you learned by observing before trying it out

Three Learning Skills: Leading, Trying and Watching

Review the three learning skills on the opposite page. Students can learn new ideas and skills in many different ways. If you understand that you have many options and learning strategies, you can use more strategies to be a better learner.

A Number the three skills as follows: 1) the skill I prefer to use most often, 2) the skill I prefer to use sometimes, and 3) the skill I prefer to use least often.

1 ....

2 ....

3 ....

B Write down an example of how you have used one of the strategies from the skill you chose as #1. For instance, if you chose Trying Learner, an example might be: I predicted possible outcomes of a chemistry experiment.

....

....

....

C Write down one way you could use one of the strategies from the skill you chose as #3. For instance, if you chose Watching Learner, an example might be: I could ask my soccer coach to show us how to head in a corner kick.

....

....

....

ideas in action

 Richard was asked by the teacher to be the leader on his biology project team. He wanted his team to do really well in their presentation on DNA. It wasn't going well.

Marta spent most of her time looking for the perfect background for the PowerPoint presentation, but made no progress on creating the actual slides. Richard knew Marta was working hard but he wasn't sure how to help. Jessi said she was waiting for Richard to tell her what to do. Pablo wouldn't come to the group meetings because he thought Richard only cared about his own grade and not about teamwork. Richard knew he needed better leadership skills.

Here are 5 Rules of Effective Leadership:

❶ The Rule of Connecting   Effective Leadership means finding a way to connect with those you lead.

❷ The Rule of Empowering   Effective Leadership means empowering others to take action.

❸ The Rule of Believing   Effective Leadership means making sure others trust you and believe in your dream.

❹ The Rule of Giving   Effective Leadership means you give credit to your team for their accomplishment.

❺ The Rule of Prioritizing   Effective Leadership means prioritizing getting the job done rather than just staying busy.

Which rules do you think are most important?

....

....

....

Explain why one of these rules is so important.

....

....

....

Which rule is not yet being used by Richard in this group project?

....

....

....

What else would you recommend that Richard do to provide better leadership?

....

....

....

....

....

....

One of the tests of leadership is the ability to recognize a problem before it becomes an emergency.
—Arnold H. Glasow

If you think you are too small to be effective, you have never been in the dark with a mosquito.
—Anonymous

 Two strong predictors of a student doing well in college are Exposure to College and Elapsed Time to College.

Exposure to College means a student is exposed to a college campus, understanding what it would be like to be a college student, and what's expected of a college student.

Have you been to a college campus before?

☐ YES ☐ NO

Do you know any current college students?

☐ YES ☐ NO

If YES, what have they shared with you about college? If NO, what would you like to know about college?

1 ....

....

2 ....

....

Elapsed Time is how long a student waits before going to college (how much time has elapsed after high school before the student attends college). It's true that there are students who return to get a college degree even 40-50 years after graduating from high school. Still, the research shows it's easier for you to make it through college if you start shortly after you graduate high school (or earlier).

When do you plan to go to college?

....

What obstacle might get in the way of your starting even sooner?

....

Start addressing this obstacle now. Possible Solution:

....

Person who can help me move past this obstacle:

....

Choose your two favorite strategies.

☐ go on a tour of a college campus

☐ talk to some college students about college

☐ talk to a counselor about college campuses

☐ go online to learn more about college expectations

☐ find out the typical entry requirements for college

☐ research "college culture" to see what's expected in college

☐ write down a college plan that covers the first 2 years

Pick two and take action! Get ready for college.

> Don't wait until everything is just right. It will never be perfect. Get started now.
> —Mark Victor Hansen

Employers want their employees to see the big picture. If their sales are expanding in South America, they want all their employees, in every department, to understand why. They want employees to know the company's priorities.

It's not much help to the company for you to focus on selling more popcorn when their goal is to increase lemonade sales. The decisions made by employees in every area of the company have an impact on the entire company. Employers want employees to use Systems Thinking, to see how all the areas of the company are inter-connected in a larger system.

Practice Systems Thinking by first drawing yourself at your school in the space below. Then connect your role (student) to at least 3 other parts of the school system (for example, buses, attendance office, teachers, textbooks, cafeteria, etc.).

SCHOOL SYSTEM

Listen to *Waiting on the World to Change* by JOHN MAYER. Look up the lyrics online.

Describe what the singer is saying in the song.

....

....

....

....

What happens when you quit leading?

....

....

What happens when you quit following?

....

....

Does the song accurately describe your generation? Why/why not?

....

....

....

What did you learn?

I know you've learned a few important things!

❝ *One of the most important things that I have learned in my 57 years is that life is all about choices. On every journey you take, you face choices. At every fork in the road, you make a choice. And it is those decisions that shape our lives.* **❞**

—Mike DeWine

NEVER GIVE UP!!!

Hope is like a road in the country; there was never a road, but when many people walk on it, the road comes into existence. —**Lin Yutang**

Ask for Help

What is a goal that you have given up on because it was too challenging? Write this goal in the center hexagon. Surrounding the goal, write in the names of people you can ask for help. Ask them for help (ask all of them). Repeat until you reach your goal. Don't give up. Ask for help!

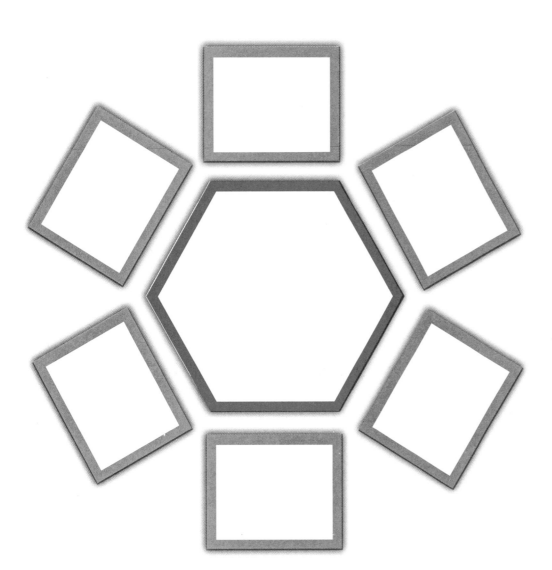

In the middle of difficulty lies opportunity.
—**Albert Einstein**

Never, never, never, never give up.
—**Winston Churchill**

The man who can drive himself further once the effort gets painful is the man who will win.
— **Roger Bannister**

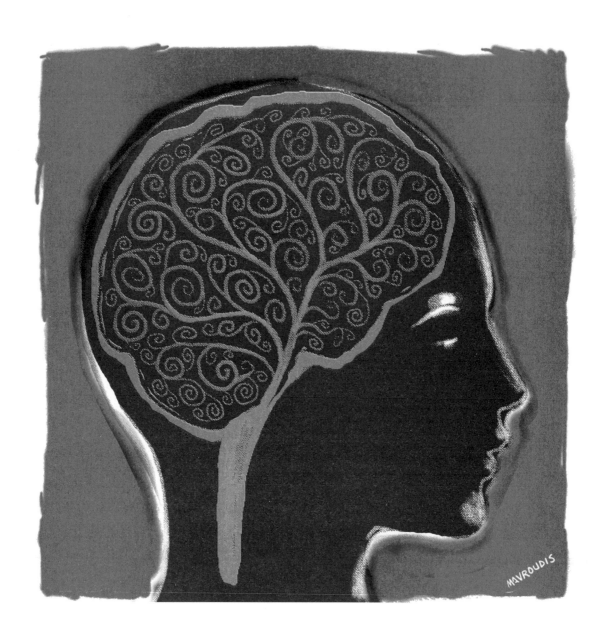

CHAPTER NINE

PAYING ATTENTION

Read the chapter to answer these preview questions.

What is mindfulness?

Why should you be able to manage diversity in your life?

What happens if you quit paying attention to your life?

How do you know when someone is a Social Learner?

What does it take to clearly see your own habits and patterns?

Mindfulness

What emotions are you feeling right now, at this very moment?

What are you thinking about right now, at this very moment?

What is happening with your body right now: your breathing, your hands, your feet?

When my sister gets on my nerves, I tell her to leave me alone so I can take a deep breath. I always use the technique when I am mad.
—Student practicing mindfulness

I think if everybody knew how to do mindfulness, there wouldn't be that much killing and fighting over little things.
—Student practicing mindfulness

I like mindfulness because it helps me feel better and teaches me to concentrate.
—Student practicing mindfulness

MINDFULNESS is an attentive and clear awareness of what's happening at the present moment, as well as attention to the future. Mindfulness means you are paying attention and have increased concentration skills. Mindfulness means you are not distracted by worry but instead are focused and feeling calm.

Students who learn mindfulness strategies reduce their levels of stress, depression, hostility and anxiety. They get along better with classmates, do better on tests and get better course grades. When you practice mindfulness techniques, you change your brain. You improve your thinking skills, become a more confident learner, make better choices and increase your ability to focus. Mindfulness can be learned in a short period of time.

On the next page are three mindfulness strategies you can try. Try them right now, each for a few minutes.

REFLECTION

Take time to stop and reflect on something you have just experienced. No hurry. What did you learn? How did you feel? Write it all down, or just sit and reflect.

CALMING THE MIND

Before a test or presentation, stop everything. Breathe deeply. Focus lightly on your breathing, letting everything else go. Thoughts can come and go. Allow your muscles to relax. Stay silent, pay attention to your breathing and do nothing else.

OBSERVATION

Stop doing things and watch what's around you. See what people do. Watch their faces, their feet. Listen to what they are saying, and how they are saying it. What else can you see? Pay attention. Allow yourself to see what you've never seen before.

Focus & Attention

If you want to increase your Focus & Attention, try these five strategies.

Get Enough Sleep Research shows that students who don't get enough sleep can't keep their full attention on learning tasks. Most teenagers need about nine hours of sleep every night. How much sleep are you getting? One measure of enough sleep is whether or not you can stay focused and attentive during the entire school day.

Pay Attention to What's Important If you give your entire focus to playing a video game every day for 7 hours, you may well become an expert video gamer. If this is your only and most important goal, this is where you want to place your entire focus and attention. However, since more than 99% of the jobs you apply for do not involve playing video games for the entire day, this may not be a skill where you wish to place your primary focus. Stay focused, with precision, on doing what is most important to you. Do not allow yourself to be pulled away from your priorities.

Avoid Distractions Many students lose focus when studying because they do not avoid interruptions. Focused students use all of these strategies: turn off your cell phone; turn off the television; don't do non-homework chatting or messaging; find a quiet place to study, in your home or at the library, and ask not to be interrupted; have a snack handy; get everything you need together before you begin studying.

You can observe a lot by watching.

—Yogi Berra

The most precious gift we can offer anyone is our attention.

—Thich Nhat Hanh

The successful warrior is the average man, with laser-like focus.

—Bruce Lee

Focus on a Single Task Do only one thing at a time. Most students are not capable of multi-tasking and staying focused. Do not try to study for your biology test, decorate your room and design a poster for a school project. Some students lose focus because of worrying about a problem and trying to solve the problem while studying. Write down the problem on a piece of paper and promise yourself you'll return to it later. Then return your focus to your studying.

Take Breaks It is hard for most students to maintain focus for longer than 45-50 minutes. Stop, take a break for 10 minutes, move around (a lot), do something completely unrelated to your studying, then return and focus again.

GOT MINDFULNESS?

Focusing on the cartoon panel, write down everything you notice about this panel. Set a timer for five minutes and see if you can stay focused for five full minutes, without interruption. Focus on this activity and nothing else. Write down *everything* you notice.

Habits & Patterns

Sometimes students cannot accomplish what they intend because they are trapped in unproductive habits. If you have gotten used to starting your homework at 9 p.m., then every night you might end up staying up later than you want. You might end up feeling frantic because you don't have enough time to finish your work. You might be frustrated because you aren't doing well on tests because you haven't studied enough and because you were up too late, and then you were too tired to focus on the test. It's just a bad habit (a "bad" habit because you aren't getting the results you want).

 Paying attention to your bad habits will help you spot which ones need to be changed.

Complete the sentence stems below, identifying some of your "bad" habits, ones that may need to be changed if you want to get better results. For example:

I'm in the habit of waking up too late to get to school on time; telling myself I'm not good at math; forgetting to bring my geometry textbook to school on Tuesdays.

I'm in the habit of ....

....

I'm in the habit of ....

....

I'm in the habit of ....

....

I'm in the habit of ....

....

I'm in the habit of ....

....

I'm in the habit of ....

....

A nail is driven out by another nail. Habit is overcome by habit.
—Desiderius Erasmus

Bad habits are like a comfortable bed, easy to get into, but hard to get out of.
—Anonymous

Bad habits are easier to abandon today than tomorrow.
—Yiddish Proverb

Habits & Patterns

 In order to see your habits and patterns, you need to know how much time you spend each day on the things you do most often.

Divide the Current Pattern pie chart below into slices that represent what you do from 7 a.m. until 9 p.m. of your typical day. The bigger the slice, the more time you spend on that activity.

Then fill out the second pie chart (Better Pattern). Each new slice should represent how much time you really should be spending on each activity. Ideally, bad habits would receive a smaller slice of your day, and positive habits a bigger slice. If you were to follow the better pattern, you would reach more of your goals and dreams.

CURRENT PATTERN

BETTER PATTERN

*Learning how to be still,
to really be still and
let life happen — that
stillness becomes a
radiance.*
—Morgan Freeman

Mindfulness

What's the Point?

Write down 2 main points from this chapter (here or in your Road Log).

1 ....
....

2 ....
....
....

Create Your Road Log

Please record your learning and ideas in your Road Log.

If someone asked you to explain focus and attention,
write down how you would respond.

Three Learning Skills

As a SOCIAL LEARNER, you learn well when you are focused on group connections, for example:

- preferring to be in larger groups of students for most activities

- feeling energized when engaged in teamwork

- valuing joining school clubs or organizations

- attending or volunteering at many school events

- speaking to or performing in front of large groups of students

As a ONE-ON-ONE LEARNER, you learn well when you are focused on interacting with one person at a time, for example:

- connecting with only a few close friends during the day

- having a favorite teacher to visit during a break

- stopping in regularly to see a school or college counselor

- having strong feelings and being very connected to an idea or discussion

- preferring to work with only one partner in an activity

As a NEED-BASED LEARNER, you learn well when you are focused on meeting your basic needs first, for example:

- bringing a warm jacket to school on a cold day

- valuing a safe learning environment

- making sure you get lunch before your next period class

- remembering to bring money to buy a ticket for a school event

- acting on learning goals to ensure that you achieve them

Three Learning Skills: Social, One-on-One, Need-Based

Review the three learning skills on the opposite page. Students can learn new ideas and skills in many different ways. If you understand that you have many options and learning strategies, you can use more strategies to be a better learner.

A Number the three skills as follows: 1) the skill I prefer to use most often, 2) the skill I prefer to use sometimes, and 3) the skill I prefer to use least often.

1 ....

2 ....

3 ....

B Write down an example of how you used one of the strategies from the skill you chose as #1. For instance, if you chose Need-Based Learner, an example might be: I made sure I brought a big lunch for my longest school day.

....

....

....

C Write down one way you could use one of the strategies from the skill you chose as #3. For instance, if you chose Social Learner, an example might be: I could go to the homecoming game and volunteer to sell tickets.

....

....

....

ideas in action

Ms. James' PE class was completely out of control.

We become just by performing just action, brave by performing brave action.

—Aristotle

Delilah read her texts while she ignored Ms. James' request for her to join her classmates in stretching. Shannon was so nervous before a scrimmage that she would run around and push other students until someone fell down. Myisha laid down after one lap around the field and said she was too tired to run. Javier ran around the field completely ignoring Ms. James' directions.

Now that you're an expert on mindfulness, what strategies would you suggest Ms. James recommend to her students to improve their performance? What strategies would you recommend from previous chapters to help this situation?

Mindfulness Strategies:

1 ....

2 ....

3 ....

4 ....

Other Strategies:

1 ....

2 ....

3 ....

4 ....

> Discipline is the refining fire by which talent becomes ability.
> —Roy L. Smith

Academic Discipline

Taking challenging classes and developing mastery of your subjects are essential to getting ready for college. Your willingness to set goals, your determination to make it to college, your level of self confidence and your creation of academic discipline are also important. **Academic Discipline** has been shown to be the most important of these four skills.

Academic Discipline means the amount of effort and focus you put into your studying and work in the classroom. The word discipline comes from a Latin root word, *Disciplus*, which means student. An effective student eats, lives and breathes discipline. When they have a choice between studying for an upcoming test or watching hours of television, they study. When they have a choice between answering the teacher's questions in class or side-talking to other students, they answer questions. When they have a choice between showing up to class on time or showing up late with excuses, they show up on time. Discipline means taking consistent big and little actions to stay in integrity with your life purpose, values and goals.

Discipline includes three skills:

① Working Hard After running your fastest for 5 miles, you sweat because you've been working hard. How hard are you working as a student? Are you working your hardest?

② Giving Your Best You know deep inside whether you are giving your best, or something less.

③ Saying No There's no way to reach your most important goals if you say yes to everything that comes along. You must say a firm NO frequently to low priorities so you can say a strong YES to what's most important to you.

Identify a low priority activity that is difficult for you to say NO to.

....

....

....

Practice saying NO. Write a text to this low priority. For example:

"sry dude I have a ton of hw to do ttyl!"

"cnt rite now hv huge test 2morrow!!!"

....

....

....

....

....

....

> [Success] comes from saying no to 1,000 things to make sure we don't get on the wrong track or try to do too much.
> —Steve Jobs

Collaboration is another critical skill for the workplace. Collaboration skills (working effectively with others) include the ability to discover shared values, to accept differences of opinion, and to compromise to achieve a common goal. Since you have reached the last chapter in the textbook, you are now an expert on career skills. It's your turn to write down the reasons why you need each of these skills in the workplace.

When collaborating, it is essential to discover shared values because...

....

....

When collaborating, it is essential to accept differences of opinion because...

....

....

When collaborating, it is essential to compromise to achieve a common goal because...

....

....

The most important question to ask on the job is not "What am I getting?" The most important question to ask is "What am I becoming?"
—Jim Rohn

LIFE & LYRICS

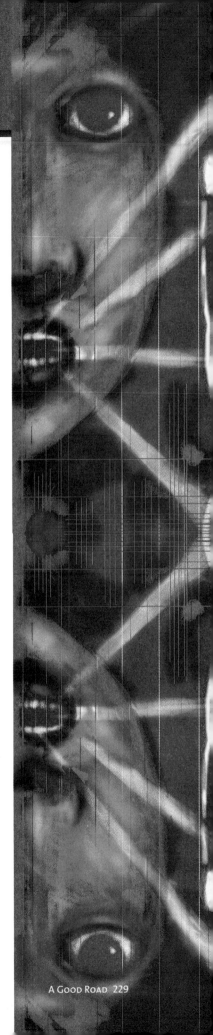

Listen to *Keep the Faith* by MICHAEL JACKSON. Look up the lyrics online.

What does Jackson's song say about the benefits of having faith?

....

....

....

....

According to Jackson, how does faith keep you moving you forward?

....

....

....

What role does faith play in your choosing a good road? Explain.

....

....

....

....

What did you learn?

I know you've learned a few important things!

> ❝ *The road I walk along is time, it's measured out in hours:*
> *And now I need not rush along, I stop to smell the flowers.* ❞

—Alvin Lee

NEVER GIVE UP!!!

 Faithless is he that says farewell when the road darkens. —J. R. R. Tolkien

Have Faith or Trust

Sometimes, when all else fails, when you have tried every strategy you can think of, you just need to have faith that everything will turn out all right. You need to trust that you have done your best. Let go of the outcome and stay positive.

Our worries about the bad things that will happen to us usually turn out not to be true. If something challenging does happen, we can't turn back the clock. Use some of the effectiveness strategies you have learned in *Choosing a Good Road* to solve the challenge.

If you cannot solve the challenge, don't give up on creating a great life. All of us live imperfect lives. We make mistakes, we wander far from a good road, and sometimes it takes time to get back on track again. In the meantime, don't forget to follow your values, accomplish your goals, enjoy yourself, and be of service to others.

 Have faith that you have a powerful life purpose, and that you will fulfill this purpose in your lifetime.

Be faithful in small things because it is in them that your strength lies.
—Mother Teresa

YOU

CROSSROADS

You stand at a crossroads. Before you are many roads to choose from.

Before choosing your road, remember the strategies you've learned. Use them. Collect new strategies along the way.

Ask for help when you get stuck. The student section of the **www.agoodroad.com** website has more ideas for you. The CGR Assessment that follows this conclusion is a great way to see how far you've come. If you need more work in some of these skills, go back to them, review them, and try again.

When you get to college, there's a great book called *On Course,* by Dr. Skip Downing, that will help you stay on course to success in college and in the rest of your life.

The truth is, life isn't always easy. Sometimes it's all we can do to just hang in there until things get better. During those tough times, you can't go wrong if you stay focused on your life purpose, goals and values.

Happy travels. Remember, whichever road you're on: never, ever, **ever** give up. **Ready, set, go!**

Choosing a Good Road Student Assessment

Score each statement below as...

(0) Never (2) Rarely (4) Sometimes (6) Often (8) Very Often (10) Always

____ Q1.   I am aware of the role that neurons and dendrites play in learning.

____ Q2.   I pay attention to my life purpose in making decisions.

____ Q3.   I have given up on goals that are important to me.

____ Q4.   I believe I can get smarter at subjects that are hard for me to learn.

____ Q5.   When I fail at something, I tell myself I'm still ok .

____ Q6.   I choose to act on my top priorities.

____ Q7.   I can come up with many solutions to a problem.

____ Q8.   I help out people around me who face challenges.

____ Q9.   I get distracted quickly when I am studying.

____ Q10. I don't know why it's hard for me to learn some subjects.

____ Q11. I forget to consider my values when I decide to do something.

____ Q12. I lose motivation to keep going when it's really hard.

____ Q13. I believe that students are only smart at certain subjects.

____ Q14. I don't believe that I can reach my goals.

____ Q15. I get busy and delay getting important things done.

____ Q16. I don't look at facts before I state my opinion.

____ Q17. My behavior is a model for others to follow.

____ Q18. When I am anxious, I am able to calm myself.

____ Q19. I know when students are verbal or visual learners.

____ Q20. When faced with a problem, I think my choices are limited.

____ Q21. My decisions are based on reaching my goals.

____ Q22. I know how I learn best.

____ Q23. I can be talked into doing things that get me in trouble.

____ Q24. I ask the teacher for help when I have questions.

____ Q25. I feel comfortable around many different kinds of people.

_____ Q26.   I have a hard time paying attention to what other people are saying.

_____ Q27.   I am very aware of what's going on around me.

_____ Q28.   I study but I can't remember a lot of the ideas.

_____ Q29.   I reflect on my life purpose before making an important decision.

_____ Q30.   I use strategies for setting and reaching goals.

_____ Q31.   It's hard for me to learn new ideas.

_____ Q32.   I avoid getting upset when other people believe negative things about me.

_____ Q33.   Because I run out of time, I don't complete important life priorities.

_____ Q34.   I have a hard time understanding other people's points of view.

_____ Q35.   I don't usually offer to help others unless they ask me for help.

_____ Q36.   I allow my bad habits to direct my choices.

Score (from 0 to 10) all the statements above (Q1 to Q36).

UNDERSTANDING YOUR ASSESSMENT RESULTS

Review sample scoring below.

Copy your scores for each of the four questions to the nine Group Sets on 236-237.

Add the two scores from the left column and write the total below the line.

Add the two scores from the right column and write the total below the line.

Add 80 to the left column total score, then **Subtract** the right column total score for a Final Total.

Scores will range from 60 (room for improvement) to 100 (very effective).

Sample Group Set Scoring

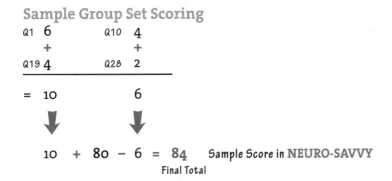

Group Set 1

Q1 _____ Q10 _____

   +   +

Q19 _____ Q28 _____

_____

= _____ + 80 − _____ = _____ Score in **NEURO-SAVVY**

• •

Group Set 2

Q2 _____ Q11 _____

   +   +

Q29 _____ Q20 _____

_____

= _____ + 80 − _____ = _____ Score in **PURPOSEFUL**

• •

Group Set 3

Q21 _____ Q3 _____

   +   +

Q30 _____ Q12 _____

_____

= _____ + 80 − _____ = _____ Score in **RESILIENT**

• •

Group Set 4

Q4 _____ Q13 _____

   +   +

Q22 _____ Q31 _____

_____

= _____ + 80 − _____ = _____ Score in **BROADLY INTELLIGENT**

• •

Group Set 5

Q5 _____ Q14 _____

   +   +

Q32 _____ Q23 _____

_____

= _____ + 80 − _____ = _____ Score in **POSITIVE**

Group Set 6

Q6 _____   Q15 _____
      +   +
Q24 _____   Q33 _____
_____

= _____ + 80 − _____ = _____ Score in **BALANCED**

●●

Group Set 7

Q7 _____   Q16 _____
      +   +
Q25 _____   Q34 _____
_____

= _____ + 80 − _____ = _____ Score in **CREATIVE**

●●

Group Set 8

Q8 _____   Q26 _____
      +   +
Q17 _____   Q35 _____
_____

= _____ + 80 − _____ = _____ Score in **EMPOWERED**

●●

Group Set 9

Q18 _____   Q9 _____
      +   +
Q36 _____   Q27 _____
_____

= _____ + 80 − _____ = _____ Score in **MINDFUL**

●●

Lower scores suggest that you have a great opportunity to improve in this skill. All of us have much to learn in each of these skill areas, so keep practicing.

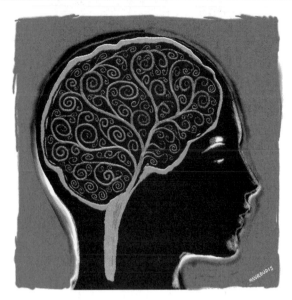
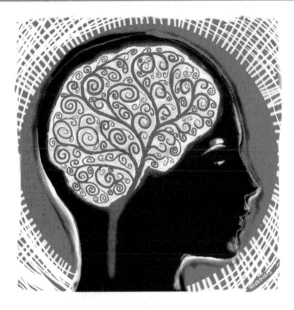
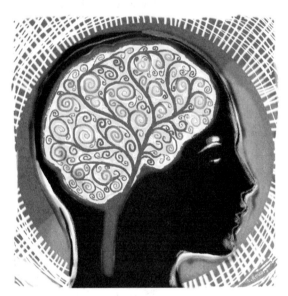
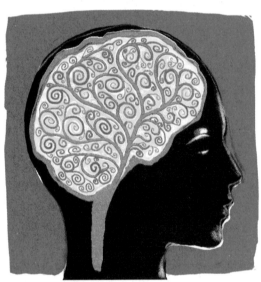

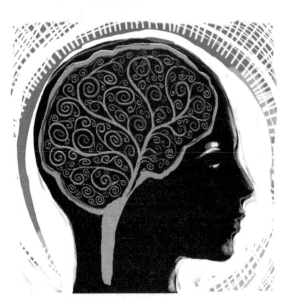